STEEL ANGELS

STEEL ANGELS

The personal qualities of a priest

Magdalen Smith

First published in Great Britain in 2014

Society for Promoting Christian Knowledge
36 Causton Street
London SW1P 4ST
www.spckpublishing.co.uk

British Library Cataloguing-in-Publication Data
A catalogue record for this book is available from the British Library

ISBN 978–0–281–07222–4
eBook ISBN 978–0–281–07223–1

Typeset by Graphicraft Limited, Hong Kong
First printed in Great Britain by Ashford Colour Press

eBook by Graphicraft Limited, Hong Kong

For my parents
Martin (1915–86)
and Monica Thornton

Contents

Contents

Acknowledgements

There are a few people who deserve special thanks on what is a very new but exciting journey.

The Revd John Lees, my friend and colleague, for encouraging me to send early chapters out to publishers and for his continual support and affirmation to me as priest and person.

Ruth McCurry at SPCK, who believed in the concept for the book and has been so helpful and positive throughout.

The Revd Stephen Edwards, whose model of priesthood and friendship I continue to find holy and inspiring.

The parish of Wilmslow, for the stories and people it has given me for some of the content for this book. For my congregation's excitement about this.

Flo Knowles, for her help emotionally and practically.

And, as always, to my wonderful family, to Eve (who was so enthusiastic when I read her parts of the script) and Aidan; and to my soul mate, best friend and husband, Paul, my scholarly 'walking concordance', for giving me space and time to write and who has relished the new flourishing in this area of my life and ministry.

Introduction

I love a good Bond film. Archetypically suave in black suit and with unshakeable demeanour, James Bond has been part of the British fictional experience for over 60 years. As the years go by the figure of Bond is continually reinvented, bringing the character to contemporary audiences – a new spirit to an old 'institution'. Different actors bring their own interpretation to this instantly recognizable yet most elusive of characters. Bond has something of an old-fashioned glamour about him, he makes things happen, he's invincible against the most terrifying of villains and challenges. Yet all of these never deter him from his mission – usually of retaining global security or saving the world from evil and obliteration. Bond is resourceful, at times vulnerable, charming and energetic, even though he might have a lifestyle and morality that some of us might seriously challenge.

The latest Bond – *Skyfall* – was so brilliant that I watched it three times, but it sees a shift in this historic Bond, who, at least initially, is not in a great place. After a serious fall from a moving train (his 'skyfall') he retreats into obscurity until he re-emerges in M's dusky front room. Returning to duty, he's put through the inevitable paces of any MI6 agent but fails miserably – somewhere in the process he's lost his mojo. But he hauls himself back into the spy saddle and becomes embroiled in a plot to disempower the villain who is attempting to use cyber-terrorism to infiltrate British national security. However much he is physically and psychologically pummelled and scarred, there is always enough of the essential Bond to connect him with the others who have gone before – his iconic way of dressing, his ability to get out of intense danger, his cars, gadgets and favourite Martini, shaken not stirred. At one point in *Skyfall*, Bond is asked by Silva, the villain, 'So what's your secret, Mr Bond?' 'Resurrection,' is his answer.

The ability to reinvent oneself and yet also retain the integrity of what has gone before through the history of a profession is a particularly hard nut to crack. I've been ordained for nearly 18 years now and I still meet people who say to me, 'You don't look like a vicar!' I always take this as a compliment because underneath the surprise, people are trying to say, 'You look normal, approachable, maybe someone I could talk to; you're not quite what I was expecting but I like it.' Clergy are a long way from James Bond but there are some serious connections to make here. Clergy are part of the furniture of our land, for better or worse. We are still recognized by the majority of people as having a role and relevance within our communities, whatever response this stimulates. But this role is continually being reinvented as well, as we respond to a rapidly changing ecclesial environment. We too still hold something of an un-assuming authority for many, which incorporates an increasing and transparent vulnerability (maybe even an old-fashioned glamour?) which is played out in TV clergy like the *Vicar of Dibley* and, more recently, *Rev.*

But one thing seems certain, and that is that however rein-vented, disillusioned and imperfect we become, as Christian leaders we are still, for the most part, standing with our heads held high. This book is an attempt to reflect on the qualities needed for being a priest in a real rather than in an ideal Church, as well as offering reflections on how it *really feels* to 'do min-istry' in the early twenty-first century. That last statement is highly subjective, of course, but I hope that much of the earthed experience and stories will echo and resonate with many emer-ging leaders, and with those who are reflecting on their own changing leadership. Rather than being a blueprint solution for everything that is needed to be a good priest, this book offers a reflection on a selection of the concepts and qualities that make Christian leadership a continually attractive vocation. These are qualities that make such leadership a dynamic, compelling and satisfying vocational job: qualities that result in a courageous leadership, enabling us to face an ever-changing culture head-on with creativity, hope and attempted holiness, believing that faith in Jesus Christ is the ultimate answer for living a meaningful life of depth and delight.

Threaded through the pages of the book are examples from the world of contemporary visual art and film – two interests of mine, which continue to help me reflect on life and God. The artist and the priest are both expressers of what ultimately cannot be described, but both attempt to put form around the unseen in ways that can be both prophetic and sublime. In his reflective essay on Bill Viola's 1996 video installation 'The Messenger' in Durham Cathedral, Professor David Jasper says this:

> The vocation of the artist is to link the past and its inherited cultures and beliefs with the changing demands of the present and future. Artists, instinctively religious, have always memorialized the past in the present by projecting it onto a possible and hopeful future. That is why art is so necessary for the well-being and health of the human soul.

The priest uses faith for human flourishing too, connecting lived-out lives, with all their mountain-top experiences and their darkest troughs, to the story of Jesus Christ, in freshly creative ways for each new generation of believers. It is continuous theological reflection.

But more than anything, the aims of these reflections are meant to be encouragement and hope, for those embarking on a leadership journey of vigour and crisis as well as for those who have a few years' experience under their belt. What is written here is for those reflecting on what has been, as well as what is to come, thirsty for hope. These are qualities I see manifest in inspiring and joy-filled colleagues as well as in the sincere Christian folk I have had the privilege of being around. These are the qualities that will seek to sustain the Church, deepen its life and crush its despondence.

The Church of England holds nine criteria of areas for exploration with which to verify a call to ordained ministry. This book uses these criteria as a framework to explore concepts and qualities needed for Christian leadership today. Through a rightly rigorous process individuals come out at the other end of this discernment often feeling that they have literally been turned inside out – that every part of their life, past and present, has been tried and tested, like Daniel in the fiery furnace. But it remains a sign of hope that God still calls such people of excellence and humility to ordination and other leadership, people who will put everything aside in order to love their God and others in a faith environment that is far from easy. It is a sign of hope that there is so much diversity in age, character and life experience. For those of us involved in the discernment process it is an inspiring privilege to listen to the stories of vocation and faith that these folk are brave enough to put on the line. However, it is important to state that as we are holistic beings, the qualities or concepts that have been set against one criterion could on a number of occasions just as much have been set against another. As comprehensive as the criteria and process of discernment are, priesthood does not come wrapped up in neat boxes; we are complex human creatures and our inner characteristics manifest themselves in many areas of ministry and life.

A friend and parishioner wrote in a Christmas card last year, 'Thanks for being my friend and being someone I can aspire to'. Feeling continually that I do not measure up to such a compliment, her generous sentiments briefly brought a lump to my throat. For those of us who lead in a Christian context, we still have a platform and opportunity to draw from ourselves and others the mystery of the living God through a public role, to communicate the story of Jesus in an imaginative way and to unlock the spark of faith that is waiting to be lit, locked and buried within many people of our age.

This book is for Christian leaders who are and always will be prepared to say 'yes' to the exhilarating yet terrifying call to leadership. Church life and what is required to lead strongly is changing rapidly. Many of us are struggling to embrace a society where anticipated change has been replaced by change that can be described as discontinuous – disruptive and rapid. New characteristics of 'priest' emerge in pioneer ministry and are moulded to fit sometimes crisis situations. We ask our clergy to be initiators, entrepreneurs, inspirers of new ways of understanding and implementing church, and more than anything to be people who can communicate with an understanding of the culture of our day. Our task and theirs is to respond to the holy winds of change, to reinvent and yet to retain those elements within our existence that continue to give life in all their fullness. It would be arrogant and naive to claim that clergy somehow hold the monopoly on any of these qualities. They are simply offered as a reflection to run alongside the criteria that form the basis of exploring and discerning leadership in the Church of England at this time in its history. Expanded on, prayed through and lived out through one human person, they also become powerful beyond measure, a model for any Christian to aspire to.

Perhaps, then, this book is written for lay people, too, who may be confused about who they think their leaders should be and who look for clergy they can not only relate to but who can help them to look towards a future in hope. It's written for those who are open to shedding some of the old models and roles of the leadership of the past. It's written for Christian leaders who simply enjoy their humanity, those who watch Bond films and *The X Factor*, who read Shakespeare and tweet, who run marathons and go bowling, who juggle children and housework and travel the world. It's written for those happy to live their lives within a Western culture and yet who do not want to lose a sense of being prophetically counter-cultural as part of their distinctive calling. It's written by a vulnerable yet hopeful priest who is still feeling the urgent call of God and who still loves being part of the Church.

1

Vocation

———◆•◆•◆———

Resilience: steel angels

The human capacity for burden is like bamboo – far more flexible and resilient than you'd ever believe at first glance.

Jodi Picoult, *My Sister's Keeper*

The greatest glory in living lies not in never failing, but in rising every time we fall.

Nelson Mandela

Antony Gormley's 'Angel of the North' towers above the A1, an enduring symbol of northern character, gritty human resilience, yet combined with the assuring presence of a divine being. A sign of strength and reflection, it is situated in a land with a history of the rise and fall of an industrial past. The sculpture is immense; it is believed to be the largest angel sculpture on the planet and one of the most viewed pieces of art in the world – it is seen by more than one person every second, 90,000 every day or 33 million a year. Weighing in at 200 tonnes, the sculpture is the height of a five-storey building, it can withstand winds of more than 100 miles an hour; below it are massive concrete piles, 20 metres deep, which anchor it to solid rock beneath.

I love the idea of the 'steel angel'. Biblical angels are multi-faceted. They are messengers and heralds, they challenge as well as comfort, communicating strength as well as tenderness. In contemporary religious and secular spirituality they can be 'guardian' and personalized; people often relate to the idea that an angel is looking out for or after them; it connects perhaps with the human need to personalize the divine. Gormley's Angel stands definite and defiant so that drivers along the A1 cannot avoid this formidable figure, this huge piece of art. When the artist envisaged his work in the early 1990s he wanted it to be a 'focus of hope at a painful time of transition for the people of the north-east, abandoned in the gap between the industrial and the information ages'.

People have always needed and aspired to figures of resilience. Resilience plays itself out continually in contemporary culture. The BBC serial *The Village* charted the life of a rural family in Derbyshire during the First World War. Themes included the pain of parents witnessing children being sent to war, the ravages of Spanish flu and the day-to-day grind of simply making ends meet. The character of Grace (played by Maxine Peake) was an admirable one – a mettlesome woman who coped with the death of her children, the depression of her alcoholic husband, a failing farm and her family's decreasing reputation in the local community. Life was tough then, and for many in the world this is not so dissimilar to the life being lived now. For people in the West, we live in an 'age of anxiety' – where the pressures are different (but perhaps just as great) – as people search for meaning at a time where there is a collective crisis in our postmodern world on many levels. We sometimes wonder whether we can simply get through our daily lives, with everything we have to juggle, or whether we will bow under the pressure. Just surviving becomes what life feels to be about, physically or emotionally, for many people.

I am constantly amazed at people's resilience. The pressures faced by an average family seem immense and weighty. One friend was recently knocked off his bike when cycling to work. The result of this has been serious depression as well as a loss of confidence in many aspects of his life. A gifted head of department at a secondary school, he has been challenged to go through a demanding course of counselling, and is himself challenging those who employ him to recognize the effects of the accident. A few months ago he faced having to 'turn his work around within one month' in the light of a looming and unhelpful disciplinary procedure. He is the breadwinner for his family. Another parishioner is in a bad debt situation. A single parent, she holds down several jobs and has to be 'two' parents to her son constantly, with no let-up. Yet she is always pleasant, polite, laughs easily, comes to church faithfully and is always willing to help and contribute to its community life. Her resilience is not a choice – it mostly isn't for the many who simply find themselves at a point in their lives when they realize that this is just who they have become. The well of strength within her is something I admire because I know that if I were her I might not be coping so well. People keep going amid real anxieties, uncertainties and unpleasantness in a whole variety of forms. As Kahlil Gibran in *The Prophet* says, 'Out of suffering have emerged the strongest souls; the most massive characters are seared with scars.'

Resilience is also learnt. I acquired physical resilience from a variety of early experiences. My first job came at 14 – long Saturdays spent washing up in the tiny airless kitchen of a café then known as a 'Spud-U-Like', followed by the walk home. Most people understand what physical resilience is – from mothers with small children to builders – and that it is an inevitable part of life. Most of us at some point or other understand what emotional resilience is too, as we experience love and sometimes loss along the way through unsustaining love affairs or bereavement. But if we are people of faith it is through these experiences that we think out, or think ourselves back, into a sense of where God is in our own and others' lives.

In today's ecclesiastical environments, clergy need to be resilient because our Church needs constantly to be restored – physically as well as spiritually. My curacy was spent in a cavernous, concrete 1960s building which had a tiny and elderly congregation. In winter the church was perishingly cold, the roof leaked big time, and although there was plenty of love and community spirit, there were no financial reserves to fund the project. The vicar, my training incumbent, put most of her energy into fundraising for a new roof. Resilience pays off, but restoring is hard work. Anyone who has overseen the refurbishment or reordering of a church building understands this. Resilience is needed because setbacks come thick and fast, with lead being stolen, fundraising falling through, or archaeology halting proceedings.

The Bible is full of individuals whose resilience and steadfastness results in them achieving great things for others and for God. In the book of Nehemiah this theme of resilience is woven through the brokenness and slog of everyday life. Nehemiah, the wine steward for Emperor Artaxerxes, is divinely inspired to rebuild the walls of the city of Jerusalem. Local officials agree to join him in this restoration project. The book records the journey of this physical restoration. It is also the inspiring story of a tenacious man who came from a position of non-expertise and humility and achieves what he does in the face of overwhelming odds. In chapter 6 the going gets tough, as his enemies plot against him and circulate malicious rumours that the Jewish people are planning to revolt and that Nehemiah is planning to set himself up as a self-made king. Nehemiah constantly calls for God to make him strong, and by the end of the chapter he asserts that everyone will know that it is God who is the power behind the completion of the work.

Nehemiah demonstrates resilience in a number of ways. First, he takes initiative – incredible considering his lowly position in the employment of the emperor; at this point in the story he has, perhaps, everything to lose. But Artaxerxes listens to his steward and grants that letters be sent to foreign governors to permit travel to Judah. Nehemiah then inspires local officials to agree to join him with his vision of restoration. He faces potential discouragement early on when his rivals Sanballat,

Tobiah and Geshem (Neh. 2.19) ridicule him and simply do not believe that he has it in him to see through such a project. Yet the rebuilding work begins and progresses, and through it all Nehemiah draws on his deep-seated belief that God will give him and his workers success. The project is one that requires the coordination of many volunteers with the constant jeering of cynics ringing in their ears. Halfway through the rebuilding, the people of Judah use the following sentiment to strengthen their resolve in the face of discouragement: 'But Judah said, "The strength of the burden-bearers is failing, and there is too much rubbish, so that we are unable to work on the wall"' (Neh. 4.10).

Sometimes in church and secular life resilience is needed for the end completion of a task or project. After the initial exciting idea, long-term projects can feel repetitive, tedious and wearisome. Resilience, closely linked to perseverance, is not just about dealing with the unexpected crisis thrown at us as leaders but about the day-to-day grind of being there, being faithful, sometimes going over the same ground again and again in order for a project to be finished. Even work that we might understand as 'a privilege', like the taking of services or the coordinating of volunteers, can feel at times irksome and monotonous. Jean Vanier, in *Community and Growth*, talks about living in community: 'It's not hard to camp – anyone can rough it for a time. The problem is not getting the community started – there's always enough energy for take off. The problem comes when we are in orbit and going round and round the same circuit.'

But resilience can also be found in our own ecclesial communities within the cementing of community itself, embedded within the relationships of people who share and are energized by a similar vision. Perhaps this is why Nehemiah achieved so much. Chapter 3 lists the variety of individuals and tribes who worked on various sections of the wall, while chapter 10 lists the exiled Israelites who return, as well as those who financially contributed to the rebuilding. Another important dynamic bound up in the rebuilding work is the fact that Nehemiah never stops dealing with other tasks and challenges, while coordinating the wall. Chapter 4 sees men building while concurrently wearing coats of armour, arming themselves with spears and weapons to guard the wall from being sabotaged by enemies who seek to destroy it. So multitasking requires resilience too, and is maybe not such a contemporary concept; it is one that proves increasingly difficult when energy and responsibility are needed in a multiplicity of ministerial areas.

The activity of God constantly challenges us into a state of *restoring*, wherever this needs to be applied: to the divisions faced within the Anglican Communion, to the broken or fragile relationships within our own congregations, to fragmented buildings, or to the meaning of faith in an age that is confused about the significance of Jesus Christ. The Angel of the North's human torso holds the vast 'wings' of aircraft, suggesting that its strength lies in its ability to carry much more than is laid upon it. In our ministry, we too carry much that has become 'bolted on' to what was originally the purity of the original priestly calling of prayer, preaching and pastoral care; we often have no choice but to bear this new load of increasing tasks and responsibility with courage. Restoration is hard work, and today is pretty much a continuous ministry in some shape and form.

Even when the walls of Jerusalem have been rebuilt and the project completed, Nehemiah is inspired to do more. He restores the practice of the Festival of Shelters, and in chapter 10 the Israelites rededicate themselves to God's law through confession, remembrance, music and praise. Alongside all this, as the people's new leader he ritually purifies rooms that have been defiled, reprimands officials for allowing the Temple to be neglected and warns against the Sabbath becoming unholy through unlawful trading.

Nehemiah is a hugely hopeful book. Here is an ordinary man who leads his people in a particular project of restoration at a specific point in human history. Through it all, he demonstrates much resilience: in brave initiative-taking; in the completion of a long and arduous project where there is disbelief and ridicule from others who dance around the edge without ever having to get involved; in equipping himself with skills that previously did not form part of his and others' knowledge base (how could he have known about building and managing projects when he was a wine steward?); and in the juggling of other tasks that he needs to run alongside the main one of re-establishing the protection of a city.

Clergy and those who lead in church are no strangers to all this either. We too have to be people of resilience, working and living with a backbone of steel. More than strength, resilience suggests the ability to keep going, to keep bouncing back, to keep believing against the odds. The dictionary definition of a resilient substance is something that can regain its original shape or position after being bent, stretched or compressed. Those who know the film *The Incredibles* will remember Mrs Incredible's superhero ability to be stretched and twisted into a variety of different shapes in order to protect her family as well as to serve others. But she always arrives back at her original shape, even if this involves some pain. This echoes the experience of many leaders in the twenty-first century, who feel that they are pulled, stretched, and tried by the forces of church and culture while still retaining a sense of the essential beauty of who they are and what they can offer to God and to others in the fragility of their humanity.

Ministry is, at times, emotionally, physically and spiritually draining and exhausting; the reality may be that it is this *most* of the time, depending on our age and situation. But resilience is about emerging spiritually intact from a situation of depression or exhaustion, and relocating ourselves after hardship, illness or just a bad day, and carrying on. It is about being people who can become symbols of irrepressible hope for others who have little or none, whose feelings perhaps remain hidden and unidentified within them. Recently there was the earth-shattering story (quite literally) of St Martin's Episcopal Church, Dundee, which escaped with minor damage after two 1970s tower blocks adjacent to it were demolished with explosives. This tiny building became a symbol of what hopeful resilience might look like, in an area where buildings are obliterated in order for regeneration to take place (*Church Times*, 12 July 2013).

Resilience becomes a lifelong journey, underpinning and supporting the whole of our understanding of what vocation is about. Vocation to priesthood is a whole-person experience; it takes 100 per cent of our being, an ontological expression of God's call to us in potentially every aspect of our lives: past, present and future. At whatever age and stage we discover and affirm it, vocation can feel like an all-or-nothing *tour de force*, and whatever else we do – perhaps especially if we do 'do' other things (as in the case of self-supporting ministers and ministers in secular employment) – then vocation has to be a long-haul journey. In the course of our clergy life, then, we will most probably undertake many things that require a breathtaking measure of resilience, which might include anything from maintaining buildings, restoring purpose and hope within a congregation, coping with criticism, covering endless sabbaticals and interregnums, to juggling a huge variety of tasks, concerns, minutiae and worries.

Ultimately, we take as our role model the man who, like a steel angel, extended his arms wide above the world, embracing all of its sin, pain and ugliness and offered instead a heart of love. At that moment in his life, more than at any other, Jesus understood what it meant to be resilient, but through it he restored our broken world to God through ultimate forgiveness and the absorption of violence. I believe that the majority of clergy and church leaders are undeniably resilient, even if they don't feel that they are. Hiding our own steel underneath an exterior of vulnerable and human flesh can potentially represent an image that returns us to our original figure of Gormley's Angel. Being resilient is about having a 'big soul', of embracing potentially much and everyone, just as the Angel of the North holds its steely arms out to the land and people beneath it. The phenomenon of 'priest' can paradoxically and mysteriously hold together heaven and earth; an awesome mixture of fluidity as well as stability, beings who have the strength to wrestle with Jacob, yet who are, like the Angel of the North, called to embrace all who find themselves under their wings.

Presence: to jar and to comfort

We convince by our presence.   Walt Whitman

Sometimes it's a form of love just to talk to somebody that you have nothing in common with and still be fascinated by their presence.   David Byrne

For the last three weeks there's been a homeless man camping on the green area outside our local library, 200 yards from where my house is. I live near the town centre on one of its most prestigious roads. Our house (owned by the Diocese of Chester) is probably worth the best part of three-quarters of a million pounds. Recently, the parable that Jesus tells about Dives and Lazarus has been ringing in my ears. I've tried to befriend the man (Pete), who remains fiercely independent, refusing all my offers of help. Knowing someone's name, of course, begins a new relationship with them, as they cease to be anonymous and become a person with humanity, a history, past, present and future, a person with needs and perhaps dreams, just like anyone else. Rationally I know that there's nothing much more I can do for Pete if he seriously doesn't want my help. But spiritually his presence out there (last night it poured with rain all night) disquietens me; it jars my own sense of comfort and our innate desire to enjoy this; it jolts my social and spiritual conscience with razor-sharp arrows of guilt and frustration. There's even a little resentment, as his presence disturbs my feelings of 'I've done with God for today'.

The place where Pete camps at night is part of a large complex that contains Sainsbury's, the major supermarket in our town. I go there most days for one thing or another. Sometimes I can whizz in and out; sometimes the trip takes longer as I encounter parishioners with whom I am invited to converse to a brief or lengthier extent. Most of the staff know me as well – with 'God-kit' on or in mufti. Whatever the day of the week, it's productive to communicate that even as a clergy person you are a normal human being who needs milk and wine and frozen peas. I've learnt to read the quizzical expressions too – a youngish woman in black clerical gear is still a relatively strange sight, which jars something within many people. So some shoppers look, then look me up and down, and then look away when they realize that I am looking at them. Perhaps most interesting are the reactions when I am accompanied by my 12-year-old daughter. Inevitably we are talking – as parents and children do, naturally – and I am aware of people going through a whole mental process: 'It's a vicar, it's a woman, she looks young, and she's communicating with a teenager. Oh my goodness, maybe it's her child . . . then she's a mother . . . it doesn't "fit" right . . . or maybe it does?'

As a priest and human being I like 'being around', talking to the folk of our parish, including random strangers who come up to me and begin a conversation. I listen as they work hard at making some kind of connection with a church they know, relate a numinous experience they have had, or simply ask me 'where I belong'. Gordon Oliver, in his book *Ministry Without Madness*, comments that society today no longer understands who clergy are or what our role is; we are merely recognized as one kind of professional. He is right, of course, but I believe that many people do understand something of who we are and the mystery of what we believe, even if this is tangled up in the complexity of who they are too.

Our presence has the potential simultaneously to jar and comfort, depending on who we encounter and what the occasion is. We are still 'odd' and unusual (perhaps especially women clergy); many people simply don't know what to make of us or how to relate to us. Regardless of who we are as personalities, we sometimes become representative of something unpleasant in a person's history. This might be bad judgement, the moral high ground, the ridiculous or the irrelevant; we jar and clash with people's already worked out understanding of society in our postmodern and reductionist Western world-view. Yet for others there is a recognition; we are a soothing and comforting presence in the community. We catalyse feelings of nostalgia in the fact that there are still churches open and vicars working in a society that is becoming increasingly multifaith, agnostic, and fast and furious; we provide visible reassurance that somehow, somebody is trying to keep suspended a moral backdrop to lives being lived, perhaps with alternative values from much of society.

Regardless of whether any of this is actually true and whether we can fulfil those things, this is how people recognize and connect with us. However we measure up, once ordained and in licensed ministry, clergy become the public face of 'the holy' to the world. At a recent service celebrating 50 years of self-supporting ministry at Southwark Cathedral, Bishop Steven Croft stated that his three most important qualities for priesthood were generosity, humility and liminality. This third quality is about how, through our simple personhood, we invite others to explore the thoughts, expressions, memories, questions, agonies they carry within them concerning the nature and relationship we all have with God.

A friend of mine understands the idea of presence as comfort very well. Stephen has recently moved to what has been described as the largest housing estate in Europe, Wythenshawe in Manchester. Still finding his feet, his task is immense. He has a huge church building to put back on the map, as well as a team of clergy to draw together after an interregnum of three years. Despite this, he decided to begin his time there simply by inviting people into his home at Christmas for a drink. 'It's amazing what can be done with a few bottles of sherry and a packet of peanuts!' he said. For me, in my sometimes overwhelming life, this feels a huge comfort: it's a reminder that essentially I don't have to do that much to be a good priest. Stephen is very, very good at just 'being there', and at just loving people. He is and will be for many a tangible sign of God's loving presence in this place, along with his colleagues. For him this state of 'being' is about wisely cultivating 'an ability to seem relaxed; there's nothing worse than clergy wielding big diaries, looking stressed and irritable, anxious about doing everything'. He's right; this is how many people feel most of the time, and it doesn't help them to be aware of it in those who are meant to carry internal space for others.

But clergy as jarring presence is a reality too. In my curacy on a bleak housing estate, funerals were one of the main ministries. They were big business in the area; people died relatively young, often as a result of diseases related to poor diet and smoking and drinking too much, and they blamed God. At that time I was only 26. I remember standing, knees trembling, at my first funeral, looking out at a sea of 250 faces. The expression written on most of them was: 'Don't tell me she's the vicar?' I was a young, female priest, from an entirely 'other' socio-economic class compared to most of those folk – I might as well have been an elephant. My presence jarred these people; it jolted their understanding of 'Father', and it jolted their confidence in me being able to fulfil the role they expected from me, and consequently (but only temporarily) my confidence in myself. But by the end of the service they were shaking my hand warmly and inviting me back to the local club for refreshments. Perhaps at funerals more than any other occasional office our presence simultaneously jars as well as comforts.

I have just read again the story of Elijah in 1 Kings. Like many of the prophets, Elijah had a double-edged ministry: jolting people out of their complacent and sometimes evil ways of living, as well as being a source of inspiration and comfort. Right from the start Elijah rubs King Ahab and his wife, the manipulative Jezebel, up the wrong way. Simply by his presence, Elijah is a challenge to them because he repeatedly tells them that there can only ever be one God to worship. His presence and message begins to niggle so much that by chapter 18 he becomes a wanted man, challenging the prophets of Baal to a duel that has no dependable outcome. When Elijah (and God) prove themselves against the other gods, Jezebel is infuriated and the prophet has no choice but to flee for his life. When Elijah becomes despondent God encourages him by demon-strating his own presence, not in dramatic power but in the soft whisper of a voice.

For Elijah this time of difficulty and challenge can be no excuse to hide away. God calls him out of this empty place of mystery to go back to where the people dislike and react against him. He is asked by God to enter the city and anoint Hazael as king of Syria, Jehu king of Israel, and then to elect Elisha as his successor. The jarring prophetic presence will not be dimin-ished or obliterated, it seems – when prophets die or are killed more will rise up with backbones of steel and continuous words of fire. Elijah's irritant presence culminates in his anger (on behalf of God) at Ahab and Jezebel in the story of Naboth's vineyard (1 Kings 21). The story of a greedy and despotic king who tramples over anyone in his path and kills those who oppose him is one that has been played out in the history of oppressive regimes throughout history. By verse 20 Elijah can take this no more and says to Ahab: 'I have found you. Because you have sold yourself to do what is evil in the sight of the

LORD, I will bring disaster on you' (or, as it turns out, on Ahab's descendants).

While it may not take on this Old Testament extremism, our presence as ordained people will both comfort and jar others in the course of a life and ministry. This is to be expected, in unpredictable situations and in unexpected times and places. With this in mind we need to protect our inner selves by growing a strong sense of God's presence within ourselves, regardless of the reaction we provoke in others, remembering that God calls us by name and that we are precious in his sight. Our personhood is made up of the history others will never see, our present reality and our personalities – the characteristics that make us distinctly individuals. Recognizing this dynamic in our lives, directing it through an inner process of prayer, coupled with the affirmation of those who support and believe in us, is vital for our own sustainability and self-perspective. Knowing that others need us and find comfort in our ministries can potentially make us more self-important than is good for us. On the other hand, we can take too seriously the reactions of others that involve anger, cynicism or non-recognition, because we jolt something within them, and they can easily be internalized to create a distorted sense of failure or self-pity.

The word 'vocation' comes from the Latin root meaning 'to call'. It is not only God's presence that has 'called' us to this specific way of living as leaders; through our vocation we 'call' to the innermost parts of others – their surface 'issues' and the parts that lie buried and festering. Presence as priest is something we can never escape from or ignore. It is the constant opportunity to begin the God-conversation, to listen to others' stories, to detect their joys, their pain and their unsolvable problems. It means being there, as part of the furniture at functions and celebrations of successes achieved; it means being there as the holy person at life's rites of passage, perhaps particularly when people are grieving. But the jarring, jolting part of presence can never be escaped from. Elijah returned to his difficult ministry in the city, but like most of us he had a place where he retreated to, to listen to the voice of God soothing him by his presence, yet pushing him ever on.

Good art contains the ability to jar as well as to feed. The sculpture erected on the fourth plinth in Trafalgar Square in 1999 was a figure of Christ by the British artist Mark Wallinger. The work was called *Ecce Homo* (in Latin, 'Behold, the man', a reference to the words of Pilate at the trial of Jesus in John 19.5). The image of Christ shows him with arms clasped behind his back, dressed in a loincloth and bearing a crown of barbed wire on his head. Although life-sized, the sculpture looked minuscule on top of the huge stone plinth. According to the artist, the then Labour government had been coy about promoting the Christian significance of the Millennium. In Wallinger's words, celebrating the birth of Christ and 2,000 years of Christianity became 'the elephant in the room' that 'no one dared mention'; it was an event subsequently played down in a country with an increasingly multifaith and multicultural identity.

This image and the way it was presented connects strongly with the idea of Jesus (our ultimate high priest) being 'presence' as both human and divine. Because of its location many people stopped to stare and contemplate, but it was also ignored by thousands of others passing by. And yet it was there, and its memory lives on in the history of contemporary art through the recording of the resurrected purpose for the plinth. For some critics, the sculpture's diminutive size actually drew more attention to it. Part of our ordained role is to represent Christ, to and in the world. We may think we do it insufficiently, but we are called to be this presence, in paradoxical strength, irrelevance and in utter fragility. Wallinger's Christ potentially jars and confronts in spite of its outwardly peaceful demeanour. It jars just as priest does, because it asks questions like, 'Is this a man?' 'Is it God?' 'Is it both?' It was a piece of art that was perhaps unfashionably Christian at the time. Clergy are this too – unfashionable at times – yet priest as presence reminds the world, still and always, that the life of God and the power of love are always present in our midst. That is a hopeful thing.

2

Ministry with the Church of England

Hospitality: strangers in our neighbourhood

Transformation happens when we offer a free space where the stranger can enter and become a friend instead of an enemy. Such space is difficult to defend and difficult to offer. It requires a willingness to allow the other person to be 'other' – which might be neither comfortable nor convenient.

Henri Nouwen, *Reaching Out*

I think we can't go around measuring goodness by what we don't do, by what we deny ourselves, what we resist, and who we exclude. I think we've got to measure goodness by what we embrace, what we create and who we include.

Joanne Harris, *Chocolat*

Every two years, the city of Liverpool hosts its Biennial, a festival of contemporary art with public installations and events by international artists sited around the city. Exploring the theme of hospitality, the 2012 panoramic exhibition was titled 'The Unexpected Guest'. The introduction to the event said this: 'Hospitality is the welcome we extend to strangers, an attitude and a code of conduct fundamental to civilization. In a globalizing world, increasing mobility and interdependence are changing the rules of hospitality.'

As members of the Church of England we can perhaps identify with this. Our church buildings have always been places where similar 'cultures of hospitality' are offered and lived out, from the simple coffee morning to the wandering spaces that cathedrals offer their naturally large footfall of

17

visitors. We know that as Christian people we are called to be welcoming, and at a time when our buildings, as well as our leadership, communicate such contrasting messages, we know we have to think outside the box to discover new ways of providing welcome genuinely and imaginatively. Two events that were featured in the *Church Times* demonstrate something of this. Winchester Cathedral hosted its 'Symphony of Flowers' in June 2013, and Bath Abbey hosted an exhibition from the Bath School of Art and Design on the theme of 'Hospitality', something that was felt to be intrinsic to the story of the building itself. Art exhibitions are often the strings that gently encourage people into a building and help bridge the connection between history and holiness. As they encounter beauty, visitors are stimulated to think about themes that are both prosaic and spiritual, potentially taking them out and away from the immediate concerns of their lives. Behind such events is the unspoken expectation that the people who work and organize anything in church will also be people of hospitality rather than hostility.

For Christians our buildings can be both our most valued assets, with possibilities for lively worship and community events, and our biggest headaches – heritage museums requiring costly maintenance. Buildings of stone, concrete and brick are symbols of a historical past, giving a sense of permanence and stability in the midst of a turbulent society where job security is almost non-existent and family breakdown is widespread. The light provided by stained-glass windows filters in the colour that many people search for in lives that feel over-pressurized and where an insouciant boredom resides like sludge at the bottom of a forgotten pond. Many enter our buildings not quite knowing why they have come; many stay not quite understanding why they keep coming back; perhaps they do so because a sense of God's presence is glimpsed, rather than specified – 'caught and not taught'. Part of the ministry of hospitality is to respond to all of this. In the preface to the book that accompanied Bath's 'Hospitality', Alan Garrow, vicar theologian, says: 'Here is a free space – one that God holds open for us all to discover who we are and where the dividing walls of hostility, of every kind, can be set aside.'

John 21 tells of Jesus appearing to the disciples on the beach by the Sea of Galilee. The story gives us some clues about offering a leadership that includes a radical hospitality. It relates one of the post-resurrection occasions when the disciples do not initially recognize Jesus. Until John realizes it is the Lord, Jesus remains a stranger – but once recognition occurs the disciples are quickly drawn to him. We sense the urgency for their renewed need to encounter Jesus once again, as Simon Peter dives into the water to swim ashore, the remaining fishermen following in their boat. The men are then strangely attracted, and maybe mesmerized, by something and someone that feels 'familiar' but cannot yet be specified. They remain unsure that this is in fact Jesus. The moment of revealing does not come until Christ invites them to the meal he is preparing. At no point does Jesus tell them who he is, but through the sharing of the meal the mystery of his identity is revealed through a tangible experience. The satisfying of physical appetites, the raising of morale, ritual and symbol are bound up together in this event, while the real significance of it is left for the disciples to unravel. Through this encounter, Jesus offers the disciples *a new space*, where change within them can begin through the rediscovery of him. What Jesus does effectively is provide a *threshold* for them to start out on a renewed spiritual journey, and he does it through hospitality. Henri Nouwen talks powerfully of this in his book *Reaching Out*, and says that genuine hospitality is not about trying to change people but about offering them a space where soul change, spiritual encounter and development can begin to take place.

So it is vital to understand the physical spaces for which we have responsibility as potential starting (or continuation) points for those who might be open to a new encounter with God.

But, like Jesus on the beach, our churches, and our leaders, have become 'strangers in our own neighbourhoods' – a strange dichotomy. The church building may be one of the oldest and most established in a village or town, and yet also the one that to many people feels the most alien. A sense of nostalgia is often the reason for someone visiting a church – or the resulting feeling that emerges afterwards. At Christmas, for example, folk recall memories of singing in a school choir at a carol service, the magic of a Christingle service, or taking part in a Nativity play. But the nostalgia generated by church is an emotion that can be worked *with*, as opposed to dismissed as unimportant. Feelings of nostalgia are primarily about longing – the longing for experiences, maybe of safety and security, that are remembered from the past but difficult to recapture in the present. Growing a church community that can recognize and take this longing further is about encouraging people to come back to discover more. Jesus on the beach was a figure who contained something of this nostalgia for the disciples. He felt familiar, maybe even a little disturbing, in a way that they could not initially put their finger on. But through their encounter with him these disciple fishermen allowed the crucial dynamic of confused memory to connect with the sharpened reality of their lives in the present. Their need to be both comforted and energized became the new bedrock of God's vision for the world at that time, and the crucial dynamic was the hospitality of the living Jesus.

The idea of 'belonging' can be confused with people simply 'existing', lifelessly and rootless, living in a geographical place without relating or contributing to any sense of community life. The film *Chocolat* (based on the book by Joanne Harris), demonstrates this through the colourful, unconventional character of Vianne Rocher. Vianne is herself a stranger, who sweeps into a psychologically closed and stifling small French village, frozen in its inability to provide either a welcome to newcomers or space to celebrate among those who already live there.

Vianne opens, during Lent, a most exuberant chocolate shop, and with it extends an overflowing, vulnerable ministry of hospitality to anyone willing to come through her door. As the story unfolds she powerfully creates opportunities for folk to share their anger, frustration and anxieties, to realize their need to fulfil their potential, to really talk with each other and to escape from the harsh realities of their lives. We witness a stranger who arrives in a settled community and offers the means to unlock and analyse the positive, as well as the negative, undercurrents within its life.

As the 'stranger in the neighbourhood', Vianne connects with those on the margins in the community: the lonely, the abused and ignored, together with the 'new strangers' – the river people who arrive in their barges. Through her hospitality she provides shelter, sustenance, a place to laugh, a refuge, but also a place to think about and reassess the tough questions that life stimulates. She has the insight to identify and understand what people are missing and therefore needing, and what their community *isn't* providing. Harris' books often have the ongoing theme of the ministry of the outsider, making powerful connections with the ministry of the priest, who moves in and inhabits a variety of different spaces in one lifetime, as well as to our ultimate itinerant leader, Jesus Christ.

In *New Testament Hospitality* John Koenig says that 'rather than burdening or threatening us, the stranger comes to teach the deeper lessons of life and to enable ministry'. Our church communities have much deep-rooted wisdom to offer an ever-shifting society and transient population where everything seems up for grabs. This also applies to the actual people who come through our doors, who perhaps we do not know so well, who come offering rich expertise in various fields as well as a depth of life and spiritual experience. Church culture sometimes projects a kind of gloss of hospitality that masks the underlying understanding that 'all newcomers should actually play by the well-established rules'. At the 2012 Liverpool Biennial an exhibit by Tunisian artist Nadia Kaabi-Linke showed a park bench, empty yet covered in spikes, which can be seen as a stark representation of how we may speak welcome with our lips but in reality we repel others by the barriers we put up.

Our priestly identity as leaders and as 'place' is, then, at the same time both established and estranged. It means that we are not just asked to welcome *in*; we are also called to accept the invitation of others by stepping into arenas we are asked to be a part of. An article in the *Church Times* (31 May 2013) described an invitation to tea, open to all, from the York Mosque and Islamic Centre, as an act of radical welcome after the brutal murder of Drummer Lee Rigby. People attended from a wide variety of backgrounds and faith groups. For us, hospitality means going to places where we might not ordinarily feel comfortable. During my curacy, our church of St Martin's, with its dwindling congregation, was next to a large and vibrant Catholic church, St Joseph's. Two weeks after my ordination to the diaconate, Fr Vin and his congregation organized a celebration for me in the adjoining church club, complete with cake. I had previously got to know several of the parishioners from 'next door' through a joint visiting scheme, and had been asked to lead worship with Vin on special occasions. Through the building of relationships with Catholic parishioners, the singing of the Exsultet on Holy Saturday, and attending my first and only proper wake, I learnt much about the generosity of God. This was 1996, only two years after women clergy had been present in the Church of England. I still reflect on this extraordinary act of ecumenical inclusivity in a social culture where young women were not particularly highly regarded.

Last year I returned to Liverpool and visited the Methodist church otherwise known as 'Somewhere Else', which has the ministry of bread-making as its own sign of radical hospitality. Situated above a bookshop on one of the city's main shopping streets, visitors are invited to make two loaves of bread, alongside those who form part of the existing community. There is an opportunity to share prayer and lunch as well. Evangelism becomes a manageable act of friendship, as those who participate are encouraged to give one of the loaves to someone they know and to tell them about the project. In this place is lived out hospitality; the community is genuinely open to anyone: *Big Issue* sellers come up for lunch from the street below. The making and eating of bread provides the familiar link to people's daily experience, and there is a nostalgic element which connects with the present reality of our own life and faith.

In reality, hospitality is often transient. One increasing challenge facing church identity is how we create hospitable spaces for people who 'pass through' – those who may desire to be part of a spiritual community but who do not remain where we are for very long, perhaps because of loss of interest or their employment situation. This is true in my own fairly fast-paced community with many professional high-earning working people. Wealth and intelligence can equate to speed and transience, and in our town people often arrive on work contracts for two or three years, sometimes less. For centuries our churches have been at the centre of communities and attended by those who are rooted and grounded in a particular place. Exceptions are perhaps the cathedral, the student church, and chaplaincies – places where transience is a way of life and state of being. But for those in parish ministry, it can be an exhausting battle to build a sense of community with congregations that are constantly shifting. But this was the way Jesus himself operated, and how the early Church established itself. In Galatians, for example, we hear of many initial arguments between the new church communities and who they were meant to be for – Jews or Gentiles.

Solid welcome and genuine hospitality are vital for our identity and future as the Church today. Whenever I ask people what they like about coming to church (and why they stay) the inevitable answer is 'I feel so welcomed'. Hospitality is crucial;

we need to continue to discover and celebrate creative ways of providing enchanted and liminal spaces where people, like the disciples in the boat, can be drawn back to Christ to share in the ultimate hospitality which is not ours but God's to give. The story of the breakfast on the beach is about the disciples recognizing and glimpsing something of divine life which is shrouded in the sense of 'what had been'. They were given a new opportunity to re-encounter the living Jesus, as they travelled from the domain of the sea to the threshold of the shore. Our churches, and sometimes we ourselves, in our frailty and imperfection, can provide these thresholds. As leaders, hospitality is about offering the physical place of our buildings, as well as the inner 'space' of our personhood; we can both welcome the unexpected and sometimes transient guest, and also accept the hospitable spaces that others offer us.

In her excellent book *Does My Soul Look Big in This?* Rosemary Lain-Priestley talks about how we often 'recognize instinctively the places in which our souls will be liberated to thrive most fully'; we identify the kinds of environments that bring out the best in us. For present and future leaders in the Church who passionately want buildings to buzz with social and spiritual life, this could well be something to aim for: for churches to be places where God's presence can be felt, where people are welcomed, soothed, fed and challenged, where both the faithful and the occasional visitor and seeker are welcomed. This is the ideal, and always only partly achieved; but understanding ourselves as 'the stranger in the neighbourhood' keeps us rooted in the humility of hospitality.

Embrace: shades of grey

Miroslaw Balka's box of darkness is disturbing in its historical echoes but beautiful as well.   *The Times*

It takes spaciousness inside of you to give spaciousness to others.
Richard Rohr

On holiday with my family in Cornwall a couple of years ago, I took a photo high up on Bodmin Moor. The image included a tin mine, an ancient stone circle and a radio signal mast. When I looked at the picture later I realized that, quite by accident, three distinctive time periods and layers of history interwove as the twenty-first century met the prehistoric.

The Church of England is an institution with a monumental and significant history. We cannot deny or erase the darker side of what is past or the murky elements in our present experience. But the ability to critique ourselves is a sign of spiritual honesty and the beginnings of interior freedom. In the fourth century, John Cassian, in his systematic recording of the lives of the desert fathers and mothers, talked about the ability to look within ourselves before ever pointing the finger at others. These days the Church has little authority or relevance in the eyes of many and its past sins are often used to denigrate or ridicule it even more. It is an ecclesial body that is criticized constantly – for living in 'the grey', for not being definitive enough about matters of moral and ethical importance; people often struggle to understand what exactly it signifies and stands for at all. Yet when those with a public voice do make statements of authority and wisdom, the Church is accused of meddling in matters that are perceived as not its concern.

Among clergy there is often a sense of gradual discontent, feelings of being treated unfairly, of being lumbered with additional responsibility or of being used to 'plug the gaps'. With this can be an ongoing confusion of identity – are we employees, office-holders, or representatives of our bishops, muddling along as best we can? If, in the current arena of intense job insecurity and recession, we are happy doing what we do, though, the relationship between leader and those who 'employ' us can provide a healthy framework for a fulfilled working life. But for this to happen there has to be a renewed trust and a fresh, loving loyalty towards the institution and its structures, where leaders are able to embrace its inevitable darkness and imperfection, remembering the light and hope that it brings to Christians and non-Christians alike. One colleague, an MSE (minister in secular employment) with a busy professional life, commented that we have to recognize that the Church is just another flawed institution; we should never forget that God is working outside of it and that we should actively seek God in all situations and not just the ones that fit the theological moulds. Another friend, a stipendiary full-time worker, said that as leaders we need simply to 'love church life . . . It might seem obvious but I notice some clergy don't like the institutional side of things. It can irritate us all and nobody likes ritualism or clericalism for the sake of it. But an acceptance, and more importantly, a comfort with this side of things is a must.'

When I was younger I noticed that I was often angry when I left church. Angry because something hadn't been 'right', had perhaps been damaging, to me or potentially to another vulnerable person or group. Most of us have been there – we can feel frustrated at the Church's policies, at its seemingly narrow-minded theology or simply its procrastination as it debates endlessly the issues we believe are fairly straightforward. But, as in my photo, we know that we cannot have the present without having the past too. Being the established Church brings privileges and opportunities but also the baggage of legalities and the need to be patient when changes seem to take for ever to conclude. Our tradition and institution will always include significant darkness of imperfection as well as uncertainty. But embracing this side of its life with courage means that we are led into it by God in grace and humility – the very nature of the journey itself.

The imposing Tate Modern gallery stands on the South Bank in London. For a number of years the multinational company Unilever was part of a sponsorship that funded large installations in the Turbine Hall – the vast space that makes up the lower entrance area of the building. Between October 2009 and April 2010, 'How It Is' was one of these, comprising an immense steel container, with a velvet black interior, installed in this space. The work, a kind of interactive box on stilts, measured 13 metres high and 30 metres long and was the creation of Polish artist Miroslaw Balka. Visitors could walk underneath the box; and they could enter it via a ramp, into the suffocating interior of complete darkness. Considerable trust was needed as individuals groped their way towards the back of the space; everyone had to acquire the skill to negotiate the presence of others within the space, as they gradually grew accustomed to the dark. Balka's work alludes to recent Polish history, the ramp representing the entrance to the Ghetto in Warsaw or the trucks that took Jews away to the death camps of Treblinka or Auschwitz. A more contemporary association is the secret travelling of those seeking asylum, escaping their homelands in metal ship containers. In his work Balka weaves together personal as well as collective memory. His sculptures often exude a kind of mournful, elegiac quality. Jessica Blackwood, in her blog on another of his works, makes the point that Balka's pieces strongly identify with his place of birth; there is poignant reference to the painful memories of a past although they are not really 'his' (he was born post-Holocaust). She says: 'In Balka's work you get the sense that the residues of the past persist across generations and far beyond their origins.'

With our collective memory and experience of the Church and its history this is what we do too. We are acutely aware of the institution's past evils and painful struggles, which connect with those of the present even if we did not personally experience them. The shock we feel when another case of child abuse rears its ugly head is one example. The task for us is to embrace this past with courage so that we use it to transform the present in its darkness too; this is a Church truly living with honesty and in hope. Richard Rohr, the

American Franciscan priest, talks about this idea of embracing the darkness in his book *Hope Against Darkness: The Transforming Vision of St Francis in an Age of Anxiety.* The Christian vision, he says, is often described as a movement from darkness to light, whereas the reality is that darkness is always present alongside light. Grappling with the presence of the dark in the presence of light, or with 'the grey', is where transformation happens.

In his life and ministry Jesus continually wrestled with the institutions of the day, just as we do sometimes. At times he criticized these vehemently; at others he appeared to work with them. Jesus inhabited an imperfect world, living with religious authority that bullied and coerced people with their pre-existing rules. Never shying away from the darkness of life, his challenge was always, 'What are you going to do with your mistakes, your ugliness, and your mess?' Our challenge as clergy is not to create scapegoats, bemoaning the past or present, but to model a brave embrace of this 'shadowland', becoming leaders who recognize these elements in ourselves too and can show our ability to move forwards in love. As Rohr says, we can begin to hate the groups, the history and the ancestry we are a part of and we overact against them. Here, he says, 'is the refusal to carry the dark side, the dark side of our own tradition ... the way through is always more difficult than the way around. Cheap religion gives us the way around. True religion gives us the way through. Cheap religion denies the darkness. True religion steps right into it.'

Most of us, at some point, rightly question how our work environment operates, and it is part of the postmodern mindset to question all institutions. This can be true for those about to begin a vocation in leadership in the Church of England, and it often emerges during theological training. This may perhaps constitute a normal railing against the system, but students sometimes need to come to terms with their significant, yet minute, place within the body as a whole, as they rediscover a sense of perspective on their own position and relative power within an organization that has been operating for centuries. If we don't do this, we are in danger of believing that we can 'go solo', that we don't need to relate or have any accountability to our fellow leaders, their churches, or indeed the larger institution.

The parable of the Pharisee and the tax collector in Luke 18 is often used to illustrate an understanding right and wrong morality or behaviour. It is also about right and wrong attitudes. Verse 9 clearly tells readers why Jesus chooses to tell it: for people 'who trusted in themselves that they were righteous'. Most clergy, if we are honest, really honest, see ourselves as the tax collector – humble and penitent, aware of our shortcomings and our need of God. But, speaking candidly, I know that I am actually far more like the Pharisee than I would care to admit. Secretly I believe that I have the moral high ground, the radical inclusivity, the joy and hope and true good news to offer people who come into the churches where I have pastoral charge. And secretly I believe that it is the colleagues with a radically different theology from my own who 'do faith' all wrong, proclaiming the wrong theology and the wrong Jesus. Many times I have walked away from a gathering knowing I have been deeply disloyal to others whose theological views are not the same as mine. Yet underneath all this, the truth is that God has the largesse of love to include all imperfect people and varied approaches to faith in his fallen Church. Our leadership is seldom 'all wrong', just as it can never be 'all good'. We are asked to embrace those with differing theologies within our ranks because we are all part of the whole – or at the very least, to be gracious, rather than wielding the sword of unkindness and intolerance.

A few years ago my husband gave me a card on Valentine's Day. It shows an image by the German artist Peter Wever of a couple, naked from the waist up, one behind the other, in a passionate, intense and enveloping embrace. The image can be interpreted in a number of ways. It could be showing an embrace that traps, displaying a kind of suffocating possessiveness where one figure holds the other so tightly that life is squeezed out of them, refusing to let them go. Alternatively here is an utter cherishing, a sense of the heady and heightened love of one person for another, through protection, loyalty and ultimately hope.

This idea of embrace is powerful in every way. Theologically we sometimes hold on too tightly to our own interpretations of how things should be, squeezing the life out of other ways of seeing things and squashing other people's individuality. Neither should we use the institution as the excuse, holding on so tightly that God cannot be experienced by those who are looking for him within the Church's structures. Embrace begins always with arms stretched out far and wide. We are a parochial, national and international Church; our embrace to others should always be open enough to include rather than exclude. This means generously embracing everyone *within* our own metaphorical four walls – including those who irritate, offend, upset and disconcert us – as well as those *outside* of them.

In 1 Corinthians, Paul and others struggle with the birth pangs of the emerging Church community. Chapter 12 talks famously about the Church of God being one body, with many parts. I take encouragement from the fact that this 'body' of the Church of England to which we belong can remain primarily healthy, even if some individual parts of it are not. Think about your own church, of the amount of good it does and its positive ministry (not something we reflect on enough, perhaps), rather than what it *isn't* doing. The reality is that our physical bodies are never completely healthy, never completely 'whole', but they generally function and serve us well the majority of the time. This Church is vibrant, changing, colourful, imaginative, loving, varied, merciful, challenging, hopeful and brave, even if it is also dark, fallen, bruised and fallible.

One of the younger members of our church was persuaded to do the youth confirmation course this year, following a discussion about 'frayed edges'. The Church, through its theology and doctrines, should rightly have 'bottom lines' – beliefs and practices that provide those who worship and serve with reference points from which to develop their faith. We all need a certain amount of spiritual security. Bottom lines are often understood as definitively black and white, however, and certain approaches to faith might want to make them so. But there is always what I want to describe as 'the grey'. Embracing our Church through leadership means really *loving it* with a renewed sense of pride in our heritage as Anglicans. Talking about loving an institution may not be a very contemporary or popular idea, but regenerating faithfulness to this flawed and frayed Church while walking the line between healthily critiquing and lovingly embracing provides a counter-cultural model of leadership. In the rush and reality of working too hard and not praying enough, perhaps our greatest loss is missing the opportunity to tell others why we are a part of it, in a society that sends out the message that there are no longer any world-views, institutions and ideological backdrops that can provide safe reference points for people to build their lives on or gain strength from.

Kent Haruf, in his delicately crafted novel *Plainsong*, describes the ministry of two elderly cattle-farming brothers who provide a safe haven for a pregnant 17-year-old girl, Victoria Roubideaux. The way he tells of their enveloping of her as she becomes part of their well-established home, and how they bring her gently into their rough and ready world, is almost spiritual. They embrace her, providing her with a physical sanctuary, but also give her and themselves space so that both parties feel their way, tentatively, into a new relationship of love. This is surely the true meaning of embracing – that we give each other and our Church space to be ourselves, creating an atmosphere of expansiveness, openly loving, embracing the past and living courageously and realistically with the present. And even if it is dark and uncertain, grey is still beautiful as we travel towards the future, gathering our frayed edges and groping in the dark to discover the power of God within each other once again.

3

Faith

—————•◦•—————

Affirmation: naming God in Tesco

If we are looking for real heroism, the sort of heroism Jesus displayed, then we are likely to find it in some very ordinary men and women, getting on with the job of living, totally unaware that they are doing anything remarkable and completely without pretension.   Ruth Burrows, *To Believe in Jesus*

Affirmation without discipline is the beginning of delusion.
                                                                                Jim Rohn

In Christopher Jamison's book *Finding Happiness*, the author identifies a spiritual concept concerning the loss of an element in our lives, something that has been slipping slowly away from our conscious human experience, as crystal water might dry up from a mountain stream. This concept is known as *acedia*, which can be understood as spiritual 'carelessness' or apathy. Jamison believes that *acedia* plays a large part in the underlying feeling of meaninglessness and unhappiness in how life is experienced by many in the Western world today. So preoccupied are we with work pressures, worshipping our homes, organizing the activities of our children and our social lives that we have become trapped in a whirlwind of never-ending busyness. We juggle so many concerns that we have no time to dedicate to the development of any kind of inner life. This can just as easily apply to well-meaning Christian folk within our own church communities as to those who feel that faith has nothing to say to them. *Acedia*, Jamison says, can be described as a loss of enthusiasm for the spiritual life itself. The word enthusiasm is derived from *en theos*, meaning 'filled with God', and as such proves a stark contrast to this spiritual apathy and general lack of awareness of the place of God in ordinary life. Resulting from this, our society is 'full of mockery' towards those who believe that their 'soul life' is the only true reality, and needs to be listened to. *Acedia* manifests itself by filling up our physical and mental life with endless and apparent vital distractions so that we never take time to reflect and pray, or learn to listen to God in the deep silence of our beings. Worryingly, I can see elements of this in my own life too.

So where does this leave us as priests and leaders, people who as a major part of their role and work try to develop, stimulate and nurture people's inner lives? In a contemporary church we cannot stop people being busy, and the last thing we would want to do is to make 'making time' to nurture our spiritual selves oppressive – just another thing we 'have to do'. Guilt about not spending time with God is something that most clergy know about as well; but with increasingly heavy workloads it can be tempting to take a rain-check on the daily office and reflective quiet time.

When exploring the potential call to ordination, a person's faith journey forms part of the process of vocation. Those who are there to discern explore the candidate's faith journey and identify where God has been present, and where the person has been subsequently led. It's about interpreting the action and presence of God in someone's life. Over the course of my years in ordained ministry I have found that many folk are clearly fascinated by the faith stories of others, but perhaps especially of 'the priest', and particularly so of women. Questions like 'What made you go "into" the Church?' are often a starting point; I've been asked this kind of question at the supermarket checkout, at parties, sitting on trains and on many other occasions. Interestingly this often happens when people have some time to listen and discuss. Perhaps if people believe that they have no faith of their own, they want to hear from someone who clearly does. This is the exact opposite of *acedia* because it is about us wearing our souls on our sleeves, displaying who we are and what matters on the outside, even though our faith starts as an *inner* phenomenon. A way to describe this is having 'transparent faith'. We are called to have confidence in our stories, and in our current positions in the Church, but also to be humble and honest with our own insecurities and doubts. Rob Bell talks about this in terms of the conviction of faith combined with humility, being dance partners together, yet knowing that we can also never completely describe the mystery.

But it's crucial that it does not remain there. There is a lot in the Bible and theological tradition that is chewy, needs questioning and might feel esoteric to many. There is a tendency for lay people to make clergy the default option when it comes to problematic pieces of Scripture or complicated theology, with an 'I can't answer this sort of question so why not ask the vicar?' kind of scenario. It's far more powerful to encourage people, with guidance, to think theological issues out for themselves, which results in them ultimately putting belief and experience into their own words and subsequently understanding it. These days those of us in leadership could be even more proactive. We should not be the only ones to talk about our faith when questioned or challenged – we should encourage those in our congregations to be able to do it too. It goes without saying that many faithful people can clearly articulate their journeys of faith and present belief. But in our time of taking no prior knowledge for granted I experience people who regularly come to worship who are just not able to explain *why* they are in church at all, let alone what it means for them. Even for folk who have been coming to church for years this proves an awkward question. A starting point would be listening to the stories of people's experience of God: the interpretation and affirmation of where the Holy Spirit of God is working in their lives. Here is an example.

Helen is a young mum with two small children. Near our town is a huge Tesco, and Helen was there one afternoon. Those of us who have ever been shopping with small children know that it is often a far from easy or pleasant experience. Children get fractious, verbalizing this by whining or crying, and parents are conscious of the judgement of others as they proceed round the store. As Helen was shopping that afternoon, she gradually became aware of a child who was indeed screaming at the top of its voice. Helen continued shopping with her own children, but after a while, so aware of someone else's overwrought child, she left her trolley and followed the sound. She found the child (still screaming), along with a sibling and a very distressed mother. Empathizing with this upset mum, she put her hand on her shoulder and simply asked, 'Are you OK? Can I do anything to help?' The woman promptly burst into tears. Helen gave her a hug, took her to the side of the store, sat her down, looked after her shopping, and succeeded in pacifying the screaming child as well as managing her own. After a short while, all parties were calm again and the two women continued doing their weekly shop.

When I heard Helen tell this story in one of our home groups I felt profoundly moved. I explained to her that she had done a number of things. Helen suffers from a lack of confidence due to past problems of bullying at school, but using her natural empathy and generosity of spirit she was subconsciously alert to the cry of someone who was having a hard time at that moment. Having heard this cry of pain, she put aside her own needs and courageously sought out this stranger, not knowing what response she might get, offering her empathy and help. All this played itself out in a very secular environment – Tesco. I believe that Helen is a person deeply connected to the voice and call of God and that she is clearly able to listen and respond spontaneously to this; in this scenario she was living the kingdom very much in the world. But even though she is a regular worshipper in church, when I described it to her as

I saw it she looked bemused. As I have got to know Helen I have come to realize that she is a Christian who has an almost mystical capacity for prayer. Her discovery of Christ through imaginative contemplation has been really exciting to explore, although she continues to need encouragement to keep going as well as warm affirmation that she indeed has much to offer. There is room, then, to interpret, to name and thus affirm our own folk who are *already* playing their part in loving God and living a Christian life. It's not that as leaders we don't see this – it's that people don't necessarily see it themselves. Because of this we sometimes do not affirm enough, but once we put words to God's activity then it enables others to begin their own theological reflection, giving them, we hope, an enthusiastic willingness to talk about it as well.

The story of Zacchaeus in Luke 19 is a similar story of affirmation and has some powerful things to say about such a ministry. We know that Zacchaeus was not a popular man because he was a tax collector. Tax collectors at the time of Jesus were notoriously corrupt, fleecing ordinary folk out of money they could ill afford to lose. Hearing that Jesus is passing through town, Zacchaeus climbs a tree so that he can watch the day's events unfold, partly due to his small stature. Jesus spots him and asks him to come down, requesting an invitation to his house. It's interesting because on this occasion, Jesus does not actually demand that this tax collector does anything to change his life. There's no insistence on repentance, no asking him to amend his behaviour in any way, making those who witness the encounter grumble because of the seeming unfairness of it all. But within a character of dubious morals, what Zacchaeus seems to embody is a genuine yearning to experience Jesus – we sense openness even if only in the form of curious fascination. It could be that Luke offers his readers this story to emphasize that Jesus had a particular heart for those on the edge of society – those who were hated and unpopular as well as those who were marginalized through poverty. But because

Jesus *affirms* Zacchaeus' enthusiasm to see the Son of God, Zacchaeus is inspired to change his way of life and become a bigger person. When he announces his intention to give back what he has taken unfairly, 'four times as much', Jesus affirms him again by stating that salvation has arrived in the life of this altered man.

Being part of the leadership of a church community is about developing the ability to affirm people who have the persistent inklings of faith. It's also about affirming those who are not particularly gifted, pleasant or easy to deal with, as well as those who are. Affirmation becomes particularly important to those who lack confidence about their place in the world and in church, or who do not find it easy to find a place of reference anywhere else. In the encounter Jesus has with Zacchaeus we see that through such affirmation a once troubled and unattractive character is transformed. Affirmation then brings about healing too, as we name and identify the light-filled, beautiful parts of folk who can be hard work and challenging. Even the many people who are easy to deal with, who we understand to be professional and capable, also battle with insecurities deep within themselves and are often far from clear about the part that God plays in their lives. In *The Missional Leader*, Alan Roxburgh and Fred Romanuk emphasize that the Church needs 'the passionate recognition that God's (missional) future is present amongst the people of God'. They go on to say that the birth stories of Jesus, the Annunciation and other scriptural passages tell us that God's future is among the least expected people – the unconfident and those who might consider themselves the theological non-experts. But sometimes people need to be told, and to be aware of the interpretation and affirmation of others, in order to see the light; most of us need constant illumination and encouragement. The book talks about the leader's role as one that helps formulate a people among whom God's future can be identified and seen. Commenting specifically about the development of a 'missional imagination', it describes how cultivating spiritual and numerical growth through specific practices and habits of Christian life is vital. Enabling people to understand and engage with the changes and pressures they face in their lives, and creating a new culture of confident dialogue, energy and experimentation for God become key factors involved in establishing a new spirit within a congregation. All this begins with the simple act of affirming with the specific aim of awakening an awareness of a God who is actively alive and present in our lives.

Affirmation of person and story is a gift that leaders must continuously offer in today's Church, because many people begin their own faith journeys with next to no spiritual confidence, often with a non-existent background in any church 'culture'. One recent confirmation candidate admitted that she did not know 98 per cent of the hymns that we sing in church, even the ones that might be considered well known. Many of us look for the powerful religious experience, the 'wow factor', but the reality for most people is that their lives are humdrum, involving hard work, and that they plateau out on to a plain described as mediocre. Affirmation of the person and their stories, together with some interpretation of where God is within them, is about highlighting the holiness of God in ordinary life. It's about making colourful once again lives that are often far from spiritually dull but might sometimes feel this way to those living them.

Affirmation is not necessarily about asking people to change their lives (although this may inevitably happen, as it did with Zacchaeus), but about learning to understand them as multi-layered and with renewed spiritual depth. Cubism, the style of art pioneered by Pablo Picasso and Georges Braque in the early twentieth century, is considered by many to be the most influential artistic movement of the last century. In Cubist paintings and sculpture, objects are analysed, broken up and then reassembled in an abstract form. The result is that the viewer sees an object from a multiplicity of different angles but all at the same time.

Although some find such an approach confusing, the technique brings a richer understanding of the object or viewpoint in question. Helping others to understand their lives as multilayered, from a variety of viewpoints, with an experience of God weaving through all of it, is a ministry that will bear fruit for the whole Church. Affirmation gives people holy permission to constantly search for and reflect on what God is already doing in every aspect of their lived-out experience; no longer is this the sole domain of those who lead.

Perseverance: strand of gold

Perseverance is the hard work you do after you get tired of doing the hard work you already did. Newt Gingrich

In the realm of ideas everything depends on enthusiasm . . . in the real world all rests on perseverance. Goethe

The film *Erin Brockovich* tells the true story of a single mother (played by Julia Roberts) who, in desperation to make ends meet, manages to secure a junior position at a small town law firm. Erin's apparent inappropriateness for this job is staggering: her language is ripe, dress sense far too sexy – added to the fact that she has no legal qualifications whatsoever. But she befriends her boss, Ed Masry (Albert Finney), and succeeds in persuading him to allow her to investigate a case involving a multinational company, Pacific Gas and Electric (PG&E). She discovers that the company is surreptitiously trying to buy up the land surrounding their site because it is contaminated with hexavalent chromium, a type of deadly toxic waste that has been illegally dumped in the area. Over the years this has affected the water supply, resulting in carcinogenic disease developing among the local population, many of them children.

This is the inspiring story of a woman who gets a taste for justice and keeps going against all the odds because she believes in a vision for what is essentially righteousness. A key point in the film is when Erin convinces Masry that the firm should take up this case, even though it will involve her persuading all 634 plaintiffs to speak against the company. The case is completed when PG&E accept that damages are due and agree to pay US$333 million to be distributed among those affected. The film is about huge, enduring perseverance to change and see a very wrong situation put right; it proves inspiring to anyone feeling like they have big things to achieve yet have all the odds stacked against them.

To persevere means to continue steadfastly or to 'persist'. Where I live in wealthy Cheshire there is a superfluity of leisure options. Adults can fill their time happily should they not be working, and young people are offered a vast range of extra-curricular activity. My own children have been involved in an abundance of activities, from fencing to drumming to street dance. I consider their lives rich, but my husband and I sometimes have conversations around the area of 'stick-ability'; we worry about where young people will learn how to become really proficient at something, expert even. Among the myriad leisure options, God, thankfully, still features on the list, even in this sophisticated and fast-paced environment. Those of us in the business of Christian leadership know full well that we compete with all the different things that people want to do on a Sunday, and at other times when 'church happens'. Shopping, playing sport, and spending time with our immediate and extended families are perhaps the most common three of these. In my current post, over the last five years I have noticed an interesting dynamic and one that I suspect other Christian leaders also grapple with. It's exciting when people walk into church with a yearning to explore the love and life of God as they recognize that this is a missing element within their lives. Church communities that are alert will want to make sure that they know how to take up these challenges so that people can be instantly welcome, can access basic theology and can begin some sort of spiritual journey.

For the last two years our church community has run what we describe as a 'Retreat in Daily Life', for three weeks in July, where we teach the basic principles of imaginative contemplation that are associated with St Ignatius of Loyola, who lived in the sixteenth century. People are given two Bible passages and asked to reflect on them for a set time for five days each week. We, as leaders, arrange to meet each person to talk through what has happened for them during the week. It's proved an enriching experience for everyone participating; it's been a privilege for us to hear something of how people sense God's presence through the process. But three weeks is only three weeks. What is the greater challenge is the practising of the technique on a regular basis, once the novelty has worn off: of getting it into the bloodstream of a regular spiritual discipline. This introduces the question, 'How do *we* persevere in helping our folk persevere in *their* faith and on their own journey?' One of the hardest realities that clergy have to come to terms with is the recognition that the most important or mainstream motivation in our lives as leaders is not necessarily seen that way by others.

This is a huge and very real problem for the Church generally in a contemporary culture of instantaneous sound-bites, lightning-speed advertising and tweets. We are developing a generation of people who can no longer concentrate on anything for very long unless it is swift, glitzy, or technologically entertaining. The life of the Spirit, the build-up of biblical and theological knowledge, the inner life of prayer and meditation, the understanding of how church communities and their 'systems' work – all this can take a lifetime to be anywhere near proficient in, and requires much perseverance to understand. As leaders we want to establish a community of spiritual depth and sincerity that means that none of us just flirts with faith. The answer, then, lies in believing that what we offer, both in our traditions of spirituality and in our worship, are worth really bothering with. It's tempting to try to make the shop windows of our worship services all about entertainment. Parts of our 'body' are becoming so desperate to build up their congregations numerically that the theological bottom lines of the past are being swept away in order to create a very low threshold to encourage people to come together as church. Welcome and making worship 'fun' sometimes become the most important characteristics for a church community. This is fine, as it is always important to be joyful in terms of encouraging folk to step through the doors. But if it stops there, ultimately it creates a false short-term reality, as people only eventually realize that hard effort and perseverance are inevitably involved in the work of being a Christian.

In *How to be a Bad Christian . . . and a Better Human Being* Dave Tomlinson talks about three different levels of happiness in living life – the pleasant life, the engaged life, and the meaningful life. The pleasant life is based on people experiencing as much pleasure as they can. It's about finding financial security, having great holidays and obtaining all the latest gadgets. The engaged life is when people discover a sense of self-worth, using their own particular gifts and calling, their strengths and positive traits. But the meaningful life goes further. It begins when we go deeper – confronting the shadier parts of ourselves, the hurts, mistakes and failures, the cracks in the mirror. The meaningful life begins when we go beyond our own individuality and connect with something greater than ourselves because we recognize our own breakability. This latter kind of life recognizes that the world is indeed an ambiguous place – full of joy and wonder yet also of darkness and pain. It recognizes that faith at its best can help us not to be overwhelmed by the darkness we encounter, believing that we can also make some small contribution to eliminating it.

Living this meaningful life is about perseverance in the things of God. Commitment to worship is about recognizing that we are part of the bigger picture, which reconnects us with a sense of the numinosity and wonder of God. Joining with others helps us to feel loved in our own imperfection as well as enabling us to learn to love those who create friction and irritate us. It also develops a growing sense of our interconnection and responsibility towards others in a joyful and progressing community. Reading the Bible, expanding our theological knowledge, and learning to pray – simply but well – provide us with potential gratitude and joy for what is already in our lives, enabling us to move forward to forgive others. By applying our gifts and strengths for the benefit of a greater cause we discover a satisfaction that goes beyond our own fulfilment. Those of us who have been Christians for a long time know and live this out already on a daily basis. But this position has most probably taken years to arrive at and even then our achievements are tattered and incomplete. Perseverance is about helping people, at whatever stage of their Christian journey (but perhaps especially those at the beginning), to know that 'keeping the faith' requires us to be precisely this – faithful to the God of life – and that we are asked to keep going, sometimes joyfully and sometimes grindingly.

In the Mediterranean bio-dome at the Eden Project in Cornwall there is a gold mosaic embedded in the path, guiding visitors around the giant greenhouse. This is a symbol of the vital presence and life-giving properties of olive oil, which has provided so much sustenance and employment to the people of this region. It is part of the lifeblood of southern Europe, whose economy would collapse if its presence was removed. Faith in a person's life should be like this too – a constant and life-giving presence that oozes into every particle of our being, as well as one that needs to be ripened, pressed and communally celebrated in order to extract the benefits. Margaret Silf, in her helpful books on how to pray, talks about identifying this 'golden strand' spiritually as we seek continuously to see God's good power in our lives as a constant, even when there are dark clouds overhead.

So how do we encourage others to keep putting in the effort on a daily basis, so that they allow God to do this work in their lives, particularly once the excitement of faith discovery (or rediscovery) has diminished? Ruth Burrows says this:

> Perhaps earlier generations did not feel the same irksomeness in monotony; nowadays there seems a resentment against it as though it should not be, as though our interest and enjoyment must be catered for at every turn, and as if when work becomes boring, we were justified in abandoning one field of action for another.

Hebrews 11—13 speaks much of faith and its perseverance. Chapter 11 begins with a statement that faith is about being assured of the eventual establishing of something that has not yet come to pass. A collection of characters are listed, people who have achieved much because of faith: Abel, Enoch, Noah and Abraham. Verse 13 reminds readers that all of these 'greats', in spite of their immense faith and commitment to God, were still living by faith when they died, often having not received the things that had been promised them by God; but they had been encouraged nevertheless by the vision of what ultimately will be. What we can take from these tenacious characters is their immense perseverance to 'keep the faith', whatever that might have meant at the time. Here were individuals who overcame kingdoms, administered justice, shut the mouths of lions, escaped the edges of swords, were beaten and incarcerated, persecuted and made homeless. Chapter 12 begins with the famous verses on running the race with our eyes fixed on Christ. Perhaps then, a key issue for us as leaders is that we must always believe in the vision God has for the world. Sustaining this is not always easy in a cultural climate of cynicism and boredom, and when our own spiritual lives can become compressed or, even worse, non-existent. If we ourselves stop praying, we may suddenly wake up one day to realize that our own passionate vision for God's kingdom and the part we play in building it has slipped away. This is why, in these first verses of Hebrews 12, perseverance is closely connected with keeping Jesus *in sight*.

Many people look to us as their spiritual leaders to inspire and encourage them in their faith journeys. They need individuals to whom they can turn, not necessarily to hold every answer to every big question, but to feel passionate and certain about the vision of the kingdom of God, however imperfect this remains. In other words, we have to be people who cannot conceive of living without the life that faith brings, with its joy, light, sacred companionship and theological sustenance. Perseverance is about this discipline of faithfulness – a concept clearly stated in Hebrews 12: 'Therefore lift your drooping hands and strengthen your weak knees, and make straight paths for your feet, so that what is lame may not be put out of joint, but rather be healed' (12.12–13).

We live in a world that expects immediate gratification in plenty of areas of life. It is vital that while perseverance should be encouraged we must not forget that it sometimes brings pain as well as satisfaction. As clergy our work is bound up with our complete being, because it is about who we are. Without our faith we would not be doing what we do – and what we do brings untold satisfaction. It also brings problems when things get tough – when we have a bad day in our two-clergy home, we sometimes joke, 'It's just a job and keeps a roof over our head.' The message that the Christian journey is far from easy and will require effort and 'stick-ability' is sometimes challenging for people to hear, and for us to communicate, especially at the beginning of someone's walk with Christ. Ordinands know all about this: often the process towards selection conference requires much effort and soul-searching, and they may be asked to be patient on their particular pathway as formation slowly continues to happen. Perseverance in this case is about retaining clarity of our own original vision and purpose in God, and dispensing with the trappings of 'achievement and failure' language that we often fall into. But to return to the New Testament, Hebrews 13 concludes with much encouragement. Listeners are told that God promises never to leave us if we have a need for his love and try to be faithful; verse 8 reassures us that Jesus Christ remains the same yesterday, today and for ever. The people are encouraged to be steadfast and not to be influenced by strange teachings – perhaps a further anxiety for church leaders these days, as it is tempting to dabble temporarily in the plethora of 'spiritualities' that are available in the market-place of the soul.

Margaret Wheatley, the American writer and management consultant, states that even secular leadership faces the spiritual challenge of finding meaning within work, and that it is precisely this meaning that motivates people. In other words, there is an increasing desire for people to make their work matter, to themselves as well as to others. Perhaps this is why church leaders can appear to be so charismatic and inspiring when they are happy and involved in ministry that proves life-giving to themselves as well as to others. Wheatley recognizes that leadership that *serves* others brings joy too. One wonderful comment is particularly relevant to clergy and church leaders: 'I want us to be the few people who live by the values that we cherish, who do work that feels right for us even if it doesn't create enormous positive change.' Persevering is about believing when no one else does, because we refuse to fall out of love with the vision.

4

Spirituality

———◦●◦———

Extreme listening: what lies beneath

That man's silence is wonderful to listen to.
Thomas Hardy, *Under the Greenwood Tree*

Most people do not listen with the intent to understand; they listen with the intent to reply.　　　　　　Stephen R. Covey

I am staying for a few days at a small Franciscan monastery in the depths of rural Worcestershire. This simple house, with its handful of brothers, is one of the most silent places I have ever experienced. You cannot hear any traffic noise; there are no sounds of any technology even though the community is on the internet. But even here, in this stillness, there is still plenty of sound – my typing, pipes juddering, the rain softly falling, a distant plane overhead. We live in an age of rare silence, of excessive and oppressive noise. My own home can be abrasively noisy, with the television, pumping music from my teenage daughter's room, the phone, the doorbell, the sound of others who come for meetings and interviews. Church life always involves people, usually lots of them. It is often noted that there is no silence in church before services these days. People use the ten minutes beforehand (if they get there that early) to catch up with the news and gossip, as opposed to quietly preparing themselves for worshipping God. Being silent means that we face the void and listen to our own inner whisperings that normally do not get a chance to be heard.

I recently went to hear radical evangelist Rob Bell speak in Manchester. As part of his dialogue, Bell told the story of his involvement in a road traffic accident on a busy highway in the city where he lives. He described the cacophonous noise of the traffic that continued to drive past the injured person, the screaming sirens from the ambulance, and the presence of other people round about, running and panicking, as trying to be swift in finding the best way to help. But amid all the mayhem, Bell described an interesting phenomenon: 'When I was right down there on the pavement with this man, with all the noise and activity swirling around me, there could be heard a kind of silence – a hush'; he felt that God was holding and containing the situation in arms of extraordinary serenity. In the middle of this crisis of life and death, shock and panic, the presence of God was in place on the pavement of this dusty city. If we, as people of faith, have ever been in a situation where we have felt dazed with shock, pain or impact, we might just be able to understand what he means. Amid illness, blood, desperation, exhaustion, confusion, even anger, we still feel the presence or word of God, as within and without ourselves we can hear something speaking, a kind of eternal pulse, or 'hum', which creates hallowed and numinous space around us in that moment.

The criterion of Spirituality asks ordinands to demonstrate that they can hear this 'hum' in their own life, within the people they serve, and in the frenzied life of the world. As leaders we are expected to have a lively and ever-deepening spiritual life, one rooted in the experience of understanding who God is in Christ, and feeling his presence in the knowledge that we and others are continuously and deeply loved. All this involves the ability to listen to the currents that ebb and flow in and around others, our churches and wider communities. Personality tests would probably indicate that a large proportion of clergy are deeply intuitive people – a good thing, because we usually need to listen *underneath* what is going on in a person's life. Sometimes people tell us quickly and easily the things that have been burdening them, their past or present secrets, and the skeletons in the closets come tumbling out. But often it's not as simple or obvious as this. Instinctively, as we listen to another we become aware that there is more going on than meets the eye, and we need to read between the lines of what someone is telling us or how they are communicating. We can be so close to ourselves that we are not aware of what is going on within us. With those who need to talk, we as clergy need to listen both immediately and as part of a longer-term ministry, putting together the pieces like a jigsaw; we need to listen 'in and around', to the whole of a life, with its joys and its tensions.

Listening to others has also always been something that many skilled lay people traditionally do and do well. These days, listening in environments where there is so little silence, stillness or mindfulness becomes more important than ever. Several churches around the country offer guidance in this potentially powerful gift as part of their mission-initiatives. Listening, as the Acorn Listening website says, is 'possibly the greatest gift you can give to another and it is life changing'. Spiritual direction has been a huge part of the ministry of listening, for clergy and others, and it requires specific training skills and awareness. I've been one of these strange beasts – a spiritual companion – for the past few years, and lately I have begun to realize that 'holy listening', or discerning where God might be in someone's life, is what many people in an everyday parish situation are searching for as well. The concept of spiritual direction can sound strange and slightly archaic to a contemporary mindset, yet the process happens all the time, in the hushed and rushed conversations we have with folk who need to talk to someone about the nudging that God may be doing within them.

Last year I attended a vocations consultation; there was an observer present, who was also the chaplain for the conference. Brilliantly, she offered her observations on the *whole* of our experience – not just the talks and discussions but the meals we shared together, the building where we stayed and the readings we heard in chapel. It struck me how this might be described as 'listening underneath and all around' a particular situation or period of time. There was something awesome, all-encompassing and deeply holistic in what she shared, as she gave nuanced observations that might otherwise have gone unnoticed. We can completely miss the dynamics, tendencies and behaviours that go on in a specific situation, in our hecticness and obsession to be busy. Yet there are deep, powerful insights to be gained and learned if we can cultivate this practice. I would like to call it something like 'extreme listening'.

The prayer 'St Patrick's Breastplate' speaks in spiritual terms of the presence of God as one that utterly surrounds a human person on every side:

> Christ be with me, Christ within me,
> Christ behind me, Christ before me,
> Christ beside me, Christ to win me,
> Christ to comfort and restore me.
> Christ beneath me, Christ above me,
> Christ in quiet, Christ in danger,
> Christ in hearts of all that love me,
> Christ in mouth of friend and stranger.

I love this panoptic understanding of our lives being wrapped around with God. Like artists, writers and other professionals, clergy have often been among the thinkers in society, people who listen to, reflect upon and comment about what is happening in their community, as well as in the wider world. Effectively this is what the observer at the conference described above does, but it can become part of the prophetic tradition, especially when, through listening, challenges are raised and uncomfortable statements made, particularly in the life of a wider community.

In Luke 8 there is the story of the rejuvenating of Jairus' daughter, which begins and concludes around the incident where a woman is healed after suffering haemorrhaging for 12 years.

While these incidents do not specifically mention the word 'listen' there is much within them that is about precisely this. First, and perhaps most important, Jesus recognizes the extreme problems that both these women are struggling with, before he speaks to either of them and before he has even met the latter. The bleeding woman was in the middle of a crowd that was pushing and pressing in upon Jesus, all clamouring for a piece of him. Yet Jesus knows immediately that something has happened because power goes out from him. Here is someone who, amid the noisy chaos, although surrounded by demands and fuss, is aware of, can *listen* to, the quietest of needs in someone who is vulnerable. The radical and extraordinary element on this occasion is that no words are spoken. Jesus intuitively hears the numbed desperation of the woman, understanding that she needs something from him – his healing power. For those of us who are sought out by others to talk to, listening is not always about the words – it may be more about the absence of them, or a person's inability to articulate them. Here Jesus listens to this woman who had been failed by others; she had most probably been dismissed by the professionals she had seen. Clergy often pick up those whom others fail, or refuse to help – those who fall through the pastoral net. Extreme listening is about our being open to anything anyone might bring to us while remaining compassionate and unshockable. It is about our willingness as leaders to 'hear about darkness and desolation, the times of God's seeming absence and neglect', as Margaret Guenther puts it in her book *Holy Listening: The Art of Spiritual Direction*. Good listening, she says, is also about resisting the temptation of always having to offer a wise response, interpreting everything, or keeping 'the conversation' lively and interesting.

This story of the woman who touches Jesus' cloak tells us that listening is not only healing; it is also an intimate thing to do. The woman clearly wants to 'touch and go', wishing to scurry away anonymously after her encounter. We all know how powerful people's stories can be, and people often feel the need to tell them. The bleeding woman courageously brings her story of pain to Jesus and invites him to replace it with healing and hope. Listening becomes a mutual trajectory, with fluidity and interaction even if few words are in fact spoken. Guenther identifies the fact that all of us need to be listened to, and we feel pain when this doesn't happen, but often we have to sum up the courage to seek someone out to be there for us. As a leader I have regretted times when I have appeared too busy to listen properly to people who want to speak to me. And there have been times when I have had to steel myself to make time for individuals who evidently need to share something significant, at that exact moment, however inconvenient it might feel for me. Guenther says this: 'In a way, not to be heard is not to be. This can be the plight of the very young and the very old, the very sick, the confused, and all too frequently the dying – literally no one in their lives has time or patience to listen.'

It's fascinating that in both the incidents in Luke 8, Jesus himself listens to the opinions of the disciples and the representatives of Jairus, but then dismisses them. There is a potential model for us here, to listen not to the apparently obvious, 'surface' stuff, the statements people throw out without thinking before they speak. At Jairus' home, those within the room are convinced that the girl is dead, and also do not listen to Jesus. Here is the refusal to hear the truth, as well as the possibilities that God can offer. But Jesus continues anyway and the little girl is restored to life.

Rachel Whiteread is a British sculptor. She won the prestigious Turner prize in 1993 for her well-documented work 'House' – a concrete cast of the inside of an entire Victorian terraced house in east London. Whiteread is renowned for her sculptural representations of spaces that people would not ordinarily see, think about or even notice – the spaces in and around familiar domestic objects. In 'Untitled (One Hundred Spaces)' (1997) she cast the spaces *underneath* 100 chairs. Her

'Untitled Monument' (2001), the third work for the empty fourth plinth in Trafalgar Square, consisted of an 11-ton resin cast of the plinth itself, which stood upside down, creating a kind of mirror-image of the pillar beneath. 'House', in particular, makes a statement about a space that is ordinarily internal.

I love this idea of making visible, or bringing to the light, the hidden, 'negative' and unobvious parts of an object – which to the subjective eye then become something beautiful. Whiteread stimulates us to look at objects from a different perspective, exploring alternative, more invisible aspects of them. As leaders, we want to enable others to unearth, or gently describe, what is not seen or understood within them – things that may be unhelpfully festering, or elements that will bring powerful new potential to them – and this often proves transformative and life-enhancing.

Clergy have the unique opportunity and privilege to provide pastoral opportunities for people to come and talk. People need to be listened to for all sorts of reasons – sometimes, simply and literally, to unburden themselves (the original idea of confession), to let off steam or to share secrets that are weighing them down. On occasions it is the need just to talk to someone who is perceived wise or neutral enough to unlock a problematic situation with a fresh pair of eyes. There have been times in my life when I have greatly appreciated talking with someone who I am aware is 'wrapped up with God', but who does not know me well and it is quite possible that I may never meet them again. I'm amazed at how much they 'see' within me, at their seer-like perception (just as Jesus 'saw' into the lives of the two women in Luke 8) and innate ability to sum up my ongoing life and its issues in a relatively short space of time. This is what holy listening is about – listening not just to the obvious but to the surrounding life of a person, group or community. It's about listening to often-repeated phrases, to the emotions behind the words, to what is often explicitly *not* said – the proverbial elephant in the room. It's about noticing the fragile and broken pieces of a person's life – what makes them who they are – and not ignoring these just because they make us uncomfortable, perhaps as we realize that we can offer no solution to their problems. Many people shy away from listening to others these days in case they either get drawn into something that will burden them or, worse, that they will have no answers. We all know 'black hole' folk – individuals whose lives, however much energy and help you give, never seem to move forward much – and it remains good ministerial practice to be continuously aware of our own limits.

But listening is not just about bringing back life; it is about finding treasure too. As a child I was fascinated by the story *Masquerade* by Kit Williams, an artist who fashioned an extraordinary piece of gold jewellery shaped as a hare and adorned with precious stones. The piece was buried in a secret location somewhere in Britain. Within the pages of the book, through words and visual imagery, lay the answers to its whereabouts. The treasure was discovered by Mike Barker and John Rousseau in 1982 in a field in Ampthill, Bedfordshire. Just like fine jewellery that is intricate and precious, our own treasure sometimes lies buried deep within us, in the histories of who we are and how we offer this to others through a personhood that can listen well. But the real treasure is perhaps the new relationships we create with others and the tentative intimacies that emerge after good listening has happened. Listening is about us being able confidently to listen to God, in and around the obscured and half-glimpsed things that present themselves to us through those we are continuously called to love.

Joy: wearing a colourful shirt

I feel I carry a feeling of God within me. That does not make me pious or virtuous, but it makes me feel hopeful most of the time.
Mona Siddiqui, Muslim writer and academic,
interviewed in the *Church Times*

If I keep a green bough in my heart, the singing bird will come.
                                                    Chinese proverb

When Nelson Mandela first became President of South Africa he wore conservative, European-style suits in sombre hues. But as he eased into the responsibilities of his new position, custom-made silk shirts in blazing African colours became his preferred attire. Richard Stengel, author of *Mandela's Way*, writes:

> They became his signature; people called them 'Mandela shirts' and they somehow symbolized his joyful pride in his own indigenous culture and history of this tumultuous country as well as a triumph over the 27 years of grim incarceration Mandela had personally experienced in prison.

What we wear often communicates the state of our inner being – how we are feeling inside, our self-esteem and personality. As clergy we are meant to be people with a rich inner life, who pray and demonstrate themselves to be comfortable doing so. Those who pray also tend to be people who are focused, who listen, are compassionate and have an energetic capacity for life in general. Priests and leaders are called to pray – in the Liturgy of Ordination (Ordination of Priests), the bishop asks, 'Will you be diligent in prayer, in reading Holy Scripture, and in all studies that will deepen your faith and fit you to bear witness to the truth of the gospel?' We are called to pray for those in our pastoral charge, to put into place the rhythm of daily prayer, using the daily office in our lives, as well as to find ways to feed our spirituality through worship. More than this, we should be people who genuinely love to be 'in and with God', who yearn and thirst for time alone with the one who has brought us life and called us to be the individuals that we are. Our inner life should be rich and evident, infusing the whole of our being and giving us a zesty, infectious love for others that challenges spiritual boredom and rattles the cages of cynicism and lethargy. In our pressurized and task-oriented vocations it's tempting to sideline this part of our charge, but if our prayer life ceases altogether we rapidly find ourselves in spiritual deep water, becoming anxious, cynical, despondent and profoundly tired; I speak from experience. Without a prayer life we are reduced to social workers in clerical shirts, or capable managers who can organize volunteers well, keep the 'show on the road' but can offer little else and suffer an aching emptiness within. Like Mandela's shirts, our life wrapped in and around the living God should bring us and others evident and expressed joy in the widest of senses. The over-cheerful vicar can prove irritating, but we draw others to God and the life God offers if we communicate a happiness and peace in our role and personhood the majority of the time. St Francis of Assisi was one who railed against his fellow brothers having perpetually 'gloomy' faces.

Our spirituality is an aspirational concept; it tells us that human beings long for a satisfaction that cannot be found in the material world alone. We cannot help people to develop their spirituality authentically if we are not practising our own. People need exposure to the presence of God through a variety of writers, prayer methods and worship styles, and this is made more powerful by the sharing of our own experience as leaders in grappling with the 'things of God'. The simple fact is that most Christian people want to pray; they know they should pray but perhaps don't know how to, feeling embarrassed and inadequate in terms of how to do it. Sharing what we do regarding our own spiritual journeys, even in our utter imperfection, can spark an interest in others in developing an inner life that feels fulfilling and real. When we succeed in articulating our spiritual unfolding, this enables our personal experience of God potentially to connect with others, and if this begins to happen can create profound experiences for them too. This can be what keeps them coming back to church.

While some churches are increasingly creative in how they model public prayer in worship and life, many of us remain relatively conservative in our presentations of this, including what happens in prayer groups. Ways are needed to nurture people's inner lives, but they should be practical and helpful because of the pressures and time constraints presented by modern life. It's also about generating an acceptance that a spiritual life can be simultaneously an ever-present reality and a mystery that is continually unfolding within, as Mona Siddiqui suggests above. A spiritual director once told me that at various stages of life we need different methods and techniques in order to pray well and feel close to God. As we grow and change as individuals, our lives require different 'food', as demands on our time and energy alter too. A short retreat during Advent recently gave me a useful tool for ministry at this present time. The retreat centred on the renewed enthusiasm for monastic spirituality. One thing the leader invited us to do was to make a string of prayer beads, a kind of Anglican version of the Rosary. The beads have proved a tangible and methodical way for people in my fast-paced parish to use as a prayer tool; it slows them down after a busy day, and introduces an understanding of personal intercession and rhythm within a helpful time-frame.

Good prayer sustains our scorched souls, keeps hope alive and brings our communities joy. But how does joyfulness through spirituality manifest itself in the churches that we attempt to lead? Joy is far more than happiness or job satis-faction; it is the constant sense of knowing that we are loved and enfolded in God in the midst of anguish and crisis. Humour is important – although our role as contemporary leaders is not merely to play the part of entertainer. The power of laughter from the pulpit (and other contexts) is underrated in our some-times intense and crisis-driven Church. People love and need to laugh, and with this to be lifted out, even if only temporarily, of their difficult situations. This is not crass, if we do this both carefully and spontaneously. Holy laughter is therapeutic; it helps all of us to retain a sense of perspective in our lives and roles, and more often than not it is appreciated. People who can laugh within a situation of adversity herald signs of a future filled with hope in God's ultimate powerful care. If we as clergy can laugh at ourselves, this communicates that we do not take ourselves too seriously, and that we have got ourselves in perspective, displaying humility and vulnerability. Several of my congregation have recently mentioned that they are tangibly aware of the message and atmosphere of joy in both of our churches. This feels like a huge compliment (perhaps also a bit of a mystery), as it can be difficult constantly to get the balance right between challenge and solace in preaching and church life. But the presence of joy in our worship is something that our folk, with their battered lives, often yearn for, coming to church on Sunday after a hard week of juggling work, home and all the other stresses. Dietrich Bonhoeffer, who knew the extreme darkness of Nazi oppression and cruelty, talks in *True Patriotism* about joy seizing spirit, body and soul – a joy that opens doors. The joy of God, he says, 'has been through the poverty of the crib and the distress of the cross; therefore insuperable, irrefutable. It does not deny the distress where it is, but finds God in the midst of it.'

So much of what we do in church involves tenacious effort – fundraising, mission initiatives, evangelistic courses. All these things form part of our identity and positively build up our communities, but if it stops there we are making incomplete statements about who we believe God to be. Joy in church life is about organizing and participating in events that have no other object except to bring folk together to have a good time and form community; it's about being able to spiritually 'play'. In our church we have a youth choir. It's only small but twice now this group has come together with our senior choir to sing selected songs from the musicals *Noah* and *Joseph and the Amazing Technicolor Dreamcoat*; a storyteller wrote and read a narrative to connect the songs we sang. Both events were experiences everyone enjoyed. Members of the congregation were invited to be part of this 'big sing', however talented or not they considered themselves to be, as a one-off project forming part of an all-age service. In the process people naturally learned something of the colourfully convoluted narrative of Joseph. Our annual pantomime, involving young and old alike, is another example.

If there is one character in the Bible who embodies this sense of inner joy, incorporating the reality of personal pain as well as globally expansive hope, it is Mary, the mother of Jesus. The birth narratives are shot through with a feeling of profound joy which clamours for the world's attention. The scenario is this. She is a young woman who is already in trouble – she is poor, uneducated and powerless. Suddenly an angel appears in the middle of her day, telling her that she will soon find herself in the most astonishing of predicaments – she will fall pregnant and her baby will be the saviour to the world. Even in this brief encounter she already knows life will be difficult, yet she draws divine strength to steel herself for this most momentous of moments.

At this point in her life Mary demonstrates an archetypical holy joy. She has much to say to us in terms of leadership in the Church at the present time and we can make the connections ourselves. Her life is far from easy, and she carries much responsibility both in the present and into the future, but does so with inner strength and determination as well as with courage and hope. Through the magnificent Magnificat she gives praise to God for remembering her in her humble position – a verbal sign of joy. When we can praise and thank God even in the midst of challenging times, then we know that joy is truly present. Gratitude is a massive part of this too. For centuries the prayer of thankfulness has been one that sustains in the middle of the darkness of life. Recently this idea of finding things to consciously thank God for each day has been resurrected in contemporary secular life, by figures such as Dr Michael Mosley. Our joy as leaders should involve a deep gratitude for the folk in our churches, and for the things they do for God both in church and in the wider community.

But more than anything, Mary refuses to let her disadvantaged position, her apparent frailty and her humble status in society affect her enthusiasm for sharing her joy. To me as a priest in today's Church some of this feels strangely familiar. Clergy often carry much weighty responsibility, they feel fragile (even if they are not), and they have a sometimes humble and unlistened-to status within a wider forum, as they have an almost unbelievable message to share with the world. In spite of all this, like Mary, they are asked to share a joy that contains a quality and mystery that originates in a depth of worship, memory and service. Joy that springs from our love of others and of God should move us away from the mesmerizing world of ourselves, as it did for Mary, connecting us with the bigger story of God. W. R. Inge, in *Personal Religion and the Life of Devotion*, puts it like this: 'The happy people are those who are producing something; the bored people are those who are consuming much and producing nothing . . . Joy will be ours, in so far as we are genuinely interested in great ideas outside of ourselves.' This is precisely what Mary does: energized by joy, she rushes to her cousin to share the news of what God has done for her, even though she is more than aware of the thunderclouds looming overhead in the life of her son.

When I was in my early twenties I spent the best part of a year in South Africa, and lived for a month in the township of Atteridgeville, Pretoria. I stayed with an Afrikaans priest and his family. A white priest from the ancestry of the oppressor, Peter was an unusual presence in this place. He loved and served his entirely black congregation loyally and joyfully at a time when racial tension was peaking – it was during the period of the CODESA talks before the structures of apartheid finally collapsed. Peter was an excellent and faithful priest, but his was not an easy role; his family were threatened and his phone regularly tapped. A man of deep prayer and a philosophical sense of humour, Peter had a great enthusiasm for life and understood what was needed to sustain his humanity and spirituality.

He prayed an awful lot, and his folk experienced tangibly the love of God within him, which spilled over to them in their anger and frustration in the mire of disadvantage that apartheid so forcibly brought. He was also a huge lover of ice cream. Every week, he and his family, including me, would head out of the township to get large cartons of fruity, creamy dessert and sit eating it overlooking the city of Pretoria, connecting us with the symbol of the bigger picture of the plan God had for that country. Living in an environment fraught with danger, Peter's depth of spirituality, his humanity and his love for God offered something of a restored dignity to those he served in that place, through the sharing of Christ's body and blood and in joyful worship.

5

Mission and Evangelism

———•◦•———

Sacred speech: how we talk about God

So when we talk about God we're using language, language that employs a vast array of words, phrases and forms to describe a reality that is fundamentally *beyond* words and phrases and forms.

Rob Bell, *What We Talk About When We Talk About God*

Kind words are the music of the world. They have a power which seems to be beyond natural causes, as though they were some angel's song which had lost its way and come to earth.

Frederick William Faber

Since it came into existence in 2004, the Beachy Head Chaplaincy Team claims that their work has prevented over 2,000 people from committing suicide on this beautiful headland in East Sussex. According to the *Church Times*, in 2012 there were 771 searches on nearby cliffs by this team, resulting in 305 'despondent people being saved'. Anyone who has worked in a ministry involving coaxing people out of situations of fragile desperation will understand just how vital – literally – are the words that are used. And not just the right words – the tone of voice and sincerity need to be communicated with the utmost care in a critical situation.

As human beings our tongues are the most powerful communication tools we possess. For people who work in forums where words are important, however, the tongue represents a double-edged sword. The letter of James, in its well-known passage at the beginning of chapter 3, speaks of the tongue's potential and also warns of its incendiary power: 'But no one can tame the tongue – a restless evil, full of deadly poison. With it we bless the Lord and Father, and with it we curse those who are made in the likeness of God' (3.8–9). As clergy, this feels even more intensified, as the moment we open our mouths to speak, those receiving our words are already making judgements about us. We live in an overly verbose society, one that is so saturated with words in various forms that we sometimes just zone out and stop listening. We have a societal mindset where most institutions are viewed with suspicion, and we remain unconvinced by the 'big ideas' of politicians and others who have a public voice.

Where does this leave us, figures who retain something of a platform in our parishes and wider communities, leaders who are charged to evangelize, to convince others of the power and love of God among us? In *The Christian Priest Today* Michael Ramsey asks clergy to 'beware of attitudes which try to make God smaller than the God who has revealed himself to us in Jesus'. When we feel desperate to get people through the church door it is tempting to site our thresholds so low that we dilute the message of a challenging and transformative gospel. But in a world where bad and destructive speech has often become the norm, what we say about God, as well as *how* we use our speech, is really important. Speech can be damaging at a meeting when dialogue is continuously interrupted, when words are used to demonize and vilify others, whenever language is unbeautiful, and when the biblical word is twisted and interpreted to suit a theological stance that does genuine harm to the human heart.

Most clergy regularly have an opportunity to preach and teach in some shape or form. Whatever and wherever this is we are given a continuing chance to offer an understanding of God using our words. The iconic beginning of John's Gospel says that God breathes life into the world through this living Word, which is Christ himself. The words we utter should echo this window into the eternal, refreshing the truth of the gospel continuously and providing soul life for those who are ready to absorb it. What we say and how we speak depends on our personalities, what area of the country we come from, our education and theological knowledge, and even how we feel on a particular day; in other words it is affected by the situation we are in. It is also impossible *always* to be careful with what we say. But before every sermon-type reflection, as people sit down there is an expectant hush; our parishioners' presence here means that people are prepared to listen, believing that we have something to say to them. We preach in different ways – anything from using a full script to spontaneous trust that the Spirit will inspire us with the right words in the moment. As 'preacher' myself I would like this to mean several things: listeners going away feeling more illuminated about who God is and what he asks us to be involved with in the world (biblical exposition and evangelistic challenge); people feeling better than they did when they walked through the door (pastoral sensitivity); a congregation reminded that actually they don't have to do anything to be loved more than they are already (a message of unconditional Christian love). Sacred speech must also be distinctively different from the words we use most of the time, yet still be speech that connects with an earthed, lived-out life. So it's a tall order, but miraculously, those of us who lead mostly manage quite a decent job, sometimes even an excellent one.

Many of us have encountered people who have electrified us in how they talk about God, with their insights and wisdom which echo something within our own depths, enabling us to progress forward in our own theological understanding. But we may too have had experiences of people who crush us with their religious rant, with theology that fills us with inadequacy, guilt, anxiety or just plain anger. Someone once told me that they didn't consider me to have the Holy Spirit within my person – I've never forgotten that. Perhaps because most communicators of the faith feel passionately about their subject there can be the tendency to get the message across adamantly and dogmatically in our statements on what is theologically 'true'.

The Bible is full of speeches of emotive energy and insightful theology. The book of Job proves a multifaceted one, as we reflect on how he chooses to talk about God in terms of what we might offer to others as 'sacred speech'. Job's life is turned rapidly upside down; a righteous man, he suddenly finds his life's stability and bounty taken away from him and is left reeling and confused. He refuses, however, to believe that he is in a slough of despond, to believe that it is because of his own sinfulness that he has found himself in such a place. Throughout the book he is bombarded by the arguments from his three friends, Eliphaz, Bildad and Zophar, who tell Job that it must be because he has done something terrible that this is so; this was the traditional theological line of the time, and sometimes of the present too. In *God-Talk and the Suffering of the Innocent*, liberation theologian Gustavo Gutiérrez comments how damaging this kind of talk can be to those who are suffering and exhausted, to say that such a situation is somehow 'their fault'. In this sense Job's refusal to speak in a similar way remains of significant importance to the subject of how we as contemporary ecclesial leaders use speech. Our words must build self-esteem, which includes a sense of God's gratuitous love for his people, whatever their situation. People should never be made to feel worse by unhelpful sentiments and bad theology, particularly if they are already beaten down and feeling at rock bottom.

Yet, as is evident in other parts of the Bible, Job does not shy away from expressing the agony of his situation in his speeches. Chapter 3 sees him cursing the day he was born, as he moves on to make connections with others living in misfortunate circumstances. He continually lobs questions at God – 'Why is light given to one in misery, and life to the bitter in soul' – as well as stating unequivocally the reality of how things are: 'I am not at ease, nor am I quiet; I have no rest; but trouble comes' (Job 3.20, 26). This tells us, as speakers, a further condition about the use of correct language: that pastorally it is important to name or state publicly the reality of how life is – favourable or rough, but often expressed in a sense of abandonment by God when it is the latter. This remains different from actually cursing God, which Job never does. What we do with the 'naming' of difficulty is, of course, another crucial issue and as preachers of a hopeful gospel we, like Job, become involved in making decisions about how we verbalize this. The naming of the reality of life should feel refreshing in its honesty as well as pastorally helpful to those listening, even if difficult things are said or questioned concerning the nature of God. But underneath this grappling has to be our firmly held belief that the God we believe in has ultimately conquered trouble and pain and is loving and good.

Following on from the idea of naming reality through our speech is the challenge of correct apologetics. Christianity's opponents often use unexplained suffering to beat people of faith over the heads with; the 'where is God?' question means that it becomes paramount that those of us with a voice speak with faithfulness and without attempts to justify, just as Job does. Job's friends, although competent theologians, remain with the stale arguments of the past, and do not relate these to the reality of present circumstances. Job says: 'I have heard many such things; miserable comforters are you all' (16.2). This seems crucial for us too, as we take into account the situations of our folk and allow these to connect with our inherited theological positions. Pastorally, we can give those who feel bruised a new possibility to feel recognized rather than glibly placated with words that ultimately mean nothing. Rowan Williams says:

> A sermon is not a lecture, not a vehicle for instruction and nothing else, certainly not a vehicle for bright ideas and speculations. Good sermons happen when the twofold listening, to tradition and to the present, really becomes a listening to and for God, so that something emerges almost begging to be put into words.

We thus need to use our words with care, as Job does, to name the reality of life, particularly painful life, and to offer those who are listening a sense of God's future of promise, which we extract from a biblical tradition of hope.

The book ultimately concludes with the message that Job understands that the world of justice must be located in the mystery of God's domain of freedom, which centres on his expansive love. The criterion of 'mission and evangelism' explores whether candidates have an enthusiasm and the appropriate skills to preach a gospel that 'permeates thinking, prayer and action' as well as showing 'an awareness of the interaction between Gospel and culture' as described above. Bound up with this is that potential leaders need to be able to demonstrate that they can articulate their journey of faith in a way that is natural and does not embarrass others. This is about having a healthy sense of pride about our faith and inner lives, and developing the ability to 'talk about God' in a way that others can identify with, making connections and energizing them. We can be in no doubt that what we say about God, and how we do so, has a potentially life-changing impact upon others. It's my belief too that many people searching for faith actually want words that I can only describe as *sensible*. They are looking for a reasonable approach, a combination of science and faith, and ethics and morality, which dispels theologies that may have been unhelpful or extreme in their pasts and which the media often peddle. Effective and tender talk of God that goes against the flow of the ignorant and judgemental speech of many of today's public voices is a potent thing. Our words as clergy have to be 'good news' to those who listen, both in a pastoral sense and also as a challenge, so that they become part of a creative restlessness to know more of the life of God. Our words, through preaching and prayer, potentially inspire the future to be believed into being and put into practice. But we need to bear in mind that however competent we are theologically, whatever we passionately believe to be true, in the words of Rob Bell, our speech will always struggle to describe a mystery that is ultimately beyond all our words.

Sacred speech has the potential to make people sit up and listen, and more than anything, think. One reason why a film script can have a great impact is because actors are saying things that we might, in reality, have difficulty in articulating. This enables us as viewers to reflect on phrases, words, truths that echo and resonate with our lives. There is something of this dynamic going on in the sermon, the talk, the 'thought for the day', potentially even the tweet and sound-bite, where people looking for God are listening out for this kind of truth. It can feel a tough yet creative call for us as evangelists to offer words that unite consolation, humour, depth and stimulation, words that without doubt preach a gospel of reality and challenge as well as hope. We are understood to be individuals of depth; we should always have at the forefront of our minds the fact that evangelism should be good news for others, and that we articulate the inner and often unnamed dynamic of God in others and the world. It is tiring listening to people who never shut up, including clergy. People who think deeply and express their thoughts and opinions sparsely and wisely have an impact on those with ears to hear, and we should be mindful of this.

Between 2004 and 2005 artist Bruce Nauman constructed a sound installation at the Tate Modern entitled 'Raw Materials'. This work consisted of 22 sound recordings of disembodied voices; some were very simple, with just the repetition of a single word. These recordings merged with the voices of visitors, creating a multilayered texture of sound. The installation reflected Nauman's fascination with the ambiguities that language has, as well as the paradox that the cavernous space of the Turbine Hall was 'filled' with the sound of words. Ben Borthwick, the curator, commented: 'The layering of fragments of previous works to create a new whole adds to this complexity.' In other words, words from the past merged with those of the present, creating a new experience for those who visited that sonorous space during the exhibition. This is what happens with our words too – as preachers and teachers we use words that are familiar from the past yet fuse with the experience of the now as they join with current thoughts, opinions and experience to form a fresh interpretation. 'Raw Materials' was concurrently complex yet also strangely calming. The last part of it was positioned in a space that people had to walk through in order to leave the building. In the recording 'World Peace', a man and a woman recited simple phrases around words like 'talk' and 'listen': for example, 'I'll talk; they'll listen' and 'You'll listen to us; we'll talk to you'. The work was described as a resting place, but also a thought-provoking comment on global-political misunderstanding. However it was interpreted, for anyone who uses words as a didactic and persuasive tool it proved to be a reflection on the paradoxical simplicity and power of human speech.

Disturbing energy: manageable mission

The Kingdom

It's a long way off but inside it
There are quite different things going on:
Festivals at which the poor man
Is king and the consumptive is
Healed; mirrors in which the blind look
At themselves and love looks at them
Back; and industry is mending
The bent bones and the minds fractured
By life. It's a long way off, but to get
There takes no time and admission
Is free, if you will purge yourself
Of desire, and present yourself with
Your need only and the simple offering
Of your faith, green as a leaf.

R. S. Thomas

Marcus Robinson is an artist and photographer who has been based at Ground Zero, New York since 2006. Using time-lapse cameras, painting and still photography he has charted the gradual rebuilding of what will be the new World Trade Center. A recent Channel 4 documentary followed his recording of visual imagery and interviews, constructing a profound journey at this most symbolic of places. Robinson says that this experience became like 'a meditation because you are in the same place for a long time and you respond to changing elements'. In interviews with the construction workers there was the evident sense of people linked emotionally – working together for a common vision. It is clear that the task has become much more than work, as they consider themselves to be doing something sacrificial, maybe even sacramental. In the words of one worker, 'You have to give yourself up for this kind of work. I'm not a spiritual person but I feel a sense that we are part of something bigger.' Emerging out of a location of horrendous trauma a new humanity rises, a nascent vision, as well as a great pride in being a part of something that holds greater significance than the individuals who plan and build.

In this description, then, there is the sense of the big vision alongside the individual people who make up the whole, the 'believers' in the big picture. God's mission for the world encompasses these two distinctive parts too – the 'big picture' of God's kingdom and the work we do as limited but faithful people. For some clergy, engaging in mission feels energizing and cutting edge; for others it is lonely and daunting, particularly when there is so much else to simply get done. For those who might be feeling as though they fall into this latter category, feeling overwhelmed by clergy responsibilities or the onset of them, this section briefly discusses three ways of understanding mission that might provide some hopeful inspiration. For those who are already happily engaged in initiatives I hope it will still have something to say. We could be described as living in an age akin to the world of the emerging Church of the New Testament;

much of our society is slipping slowly away from any kind of understanding or knowledge of the Christian gospel. Many dioceses have been prompted to think strategically, challenging every parish to think missiologically – to explore what they can do to grow the Church. The emergence of pioneer ministry in the discernment process has challenged those who test vocation to think radically about entrepreneurial leadership at this time of massive opportunity. Terms such as 'inspirer', 'risk-taker', 'counter-cultural' challenge leaders to think outside of the well-established box. We live at a time when experiment and creativity are mostly understood as good things, whether this involves holding services in a forest or running a Christian radio station. The kingdom, as R. S. Thomas describes so exquisitely, is about the opportunities there are in the now, as well as holding on to the vision of what is not yet. That image might feel a long way in the future for those of us trying to get some initiative off the ground, but the signs of hope come in the moments of pure gold – 'festivals at which the poor man is king and the consumptive is healed'. This most visionary of poets tells us that although it might feel hard and far away, all we need is the simple offering of an enthusiastic faith, 'green as a leaf'.

Whether we see parish boundaries as a help or hindrance, for the moment they are here to stay and if nothing else they provide a geographical and mental boundary for us to serve within. Every context is different and Jesus adapted his message according to where he was. A story in Luke 5 tells of Jesus spontaneously taking the opportunity to get into one of the boats of the local fishermen so that he could teach the maximum amount of people. In other words he uses the local resources that were there – the boats – as well as the local people – the fishermen. The story relates that Jesus' presence enables the disciples, who had struggled the previous night, to catch a miraculous net of fish.

At a time when community often happens as network and in a society where Christian people tend to be busy, how do we as leaders inspire and activate those within our pastoral charge? However tight for time we are, most of us want to be relational and many feel a sense that welcome is a tremendously powerful tool to begin to create a Christ-like environment. The Big Lunch, an Eden Project initiative, aims to 'get as many people from across the UK to have lunch once a year in a simple act of community, friendship and fun'. An inspiring video talks about loving your neighbour, learning people's names and sharing at an economically tough time. We as Church also need to relearn doing mission right where we are. A similar initiative has been happening in Birmingham and Lichfield Dioceses where parish churches are the starting point for reintroducing the simple idea of old-fashioned neighbourliness. The Street Association initiative has been a way of recognizing the level of social diversity and loneliness that exists in a society where a sense of community identity often feels non-existent. Since 2011, in the Birmingham area, Martin and Gina Graham have established 32 street associations, enabling groups of 50–100 adjacent houses to re-form community (*Church Times*, 4 October 2013). One home hosts a meeting where relationships form across cultures, ages and backgrounds; social activities – walks and picnics – are organized; people feel a greater sense of empowerment in community matters. The results show that through this scheme many folk feel less isolated and happier in their neighbourhood and it is from the churches that the original enterprise came and where volunteers are often found to begin a new street association. First, then, *mission can be simple, local and can provide practical help to others right where we are.*

Jesus in the boat listened to the needs not only of the crowds but of the fishermen who were probably despondent after a bad night's catch. Although he used that fishing trip to communicate something of the coming kingdom, Jesus enabled these men to catch real fish too, which they presumably used to feed their families and sold the extra for cash. One command and one action demonstrate the juxtaposition of practical help with spiritual metaphor and symbol. His actions in this incident used his relationships with local people as well as ministering to the more anonymous members of the crowd. Jesus listened and acted locally; he provided practical help, which he used to point forward to the greater vision of the kingdom of God. At the end of the passage we are told that the fishermen 'left everything and followed him', such was the impact of the whole occasion upon them. We often respond well to getting involved in things that provide genuine practical help and support for others. These ventures become even more powerful if we as leaders can make spiritual connections between them and the bigger picture that is the kingdom of God, to encourage and inspire those involved. This doesn't have to be complicated. Two years ago in my own parish we began a food bank as a 'mustard-seed' experiment. The project, 'Food Friend', has grown, and we have never been short of volunteers; it seems as if it is easier to get people to help with the food bank than it is to find someone to clean the brass. People like to feel that they are making a difference, and mission like this will inevitably attract those who inhabit the edges of church because they understand when a project is practically making a difference where they live. In this sense such projects have a twofold impact: apart from being practical, they can be evangelistic for those who do not often come to worship.

These days there are a multitude of models that tell us how to 'do mission'. Perhaps our personalities, and the contexts in which we find ourselves, also tell us how best to approach this area of church life and leadership. Our neighbourhood may call for a radical vision to be implemented and built over years, and our personalities may eagerly relish such a comprehensive challenge. The idea of laying the foundations for faith to be built on a long-term basis is evident in many of the epistles. In Corinth Paul labours below the surface of things and his special burden in this place is to put the gospel at the heart of the community's spiritual life so that it can make sound its future stability and integrity. Part of this takes further the idea of creating relationships with people in a community. A second way mission is happening across the country is the restored connection between ourselves and others who might have need of the *physical space we might offer through our buildings.*

The beginnings of 'mission', then, might be ourselves as leaders being open to others who come to us in search of help and mutual relationships. Similarly we might feel that there is a 'need' but think we are ill-equipped to get something off the ground because we do not have sufficient expertise or confidence in a particular area of work. A connection with a newly formed town council has meant that the clerk and other staff now rent office space from us, which has led to a job club and the CAB using our premises. Links and relationships between church members and community representatives are being built up; the town council recently embraced the vision for our food bank and donated funds so that we can develop the project. This is mission, working for our town together with others who may have more expertise than we do. This type of mission is based on relationships between ourselves as people of faith and those who might not consider themselves to be specific followers of Christ. Stephen Spencer comments that healthy mission should also move us away from the oppressive obsession that church growth is equated with increased numbers. It is far more about our effect on others – how we love, serve and share Christ's love and message through this building of relationships, which may have a far more durable effect than anything else. Spencer says that a type of mission is needed that 'seeks to awaken an awareness of the presence of God within the community and to encourage the people to respond to it' (*Church Times*, 22 March 2013). For leaders facing the world in a position of isolation and loneliness, such an approach can be helpful, even if it is just linking with one or two individuals or groups.

A third way we can lead people into mission is by *making it easy for them by lowering the threshold of expectations in terms of their time*. In my own context of intelligent and pressurized professionals, many people feel as though they do not have much extra energy to dedicate to church initiatives other than coming to worship on Sundays. Ironically, being over-busy means that we can become potentially unmotivated and passive in terms of serving others simply because we believe we have no extra time. Our leadership in this arena involves discerning what is actually feasible in terms of what people can commit to. My experience tells me that members of my congregation are very good at bringing others to church just through gentle and sensitive responses to enquiries from parents at the playground or approaches from work colleagues. It is often their enthusiasm that carries weight in conversations – another quintessential New Testament characteristic of the first believers. Many writers on mission claim that this is perhaps more representative of the early Christian experience of mission than the accounts we have of the grander strategies and proclamatory visions of high-profile evangelists like Paul. Stanley Skreslet's *Picturing Christian Witness* asks us to 'look in the shadows around the edges of the New Testament narratives where hints of other evangelizers, considerably less well known, lie waiting to be discovered'. I like this because here is the basis for an accessible way that Christian people can be unselfconscious evangelists. Here is 'manageable mission'.

The story in Mark 2.1–12 tells how four friends carried a paralysed man to Jesus. A clamouring crowd of people made it impossible for them to get through the door of the house where Jesus was, and so the four thought 'outside the box' and decided that, against all odds, they would get their friend to Jesus by lowering him through the roof. Here are individuals bringing someone who has a need into Jesus' presence – this is mission through friendship and association. Here too are people taking a fresh and novel approach (in their own way) to achieve this. As Hugh Rayment-Pickard says, 'Jesus provided minimal instruction for the church; so the first Christians and their successors had no choice but to be inventors' (*Church Times*, 28 March 2013). Often people invite others when there is something to invite them to, such as events and ministries that might meet a need or satiate a sense of lostness.

Mission requires us to be creative, but to keep this within realistic boundaries for those whose lives are already overfull. On this theme I was inspired by an initiative set up by theologian John Hull called 'Justice Mail'. The website states that this is for 'busy people who want to take part in campaigns but don't know what to do', or, we might add, 'how to act politically' as a person of faith. Those who want to be involved sign up for emails and receive messages about actions, with a link to an organization such as Amnesty or Change. They can put their signature to a current campaign, which is quick and easy, and statistics show that it gets results and situations are changed. It has proved to be a process that educates people and enthuses them to go on to more serious efforts.

The experience of being leaders of a missional community needn't feel like being a rabbit in the headlights, for us or for those we try to stimulate. I have reflected on the re-establishing of the old and the initiating of new relationships, and the transformative power this has within a community. We should try to listen to the needs within a community and link with other local professional organizations to build initiatives, perhaps utilizing the physical buildings that we are responsible for as leaders. Our discernment comes in sometimes simplifying our approach to the mission we are involved in so that we do not spread ourselves too thinly. However hard the environment in which we now find ourselves, we are still charged with spreading the gospel and building the kingdom, with the help of the Holy Spirit, in the best way we can. We are charged to inspire others with ways of doing mission that feel energizing yet manageable for all concerned, partly so we push against the attitudes of complacency and hopelessness inherent in our society. Ours is an energy that must excite and disturb enough to want to be involved in the bigger vision, even if we have to accept that the part we play will be small or minimal. A church I worked at in Birmingham underwent a substantial re-ordering and the building was closed for many months. I was the organizer of an arts project there, and coordinated the making of a giant duvet; hundreds of pillowcases were distributed to individuals and community groups to be decorated with their 'dreams for a better city'. Once the pillowcases were sewn together, this quilt was used to symbolically 'wake up' the church once again after the period of closure and refurbishment. In the process people had come up with many creative ideas for new mission ventures for when the doors opened again. Mission in leadership is about stirring up the sense of discipleship within everyone, inspiring ourselves and others to wake up again and see beyond the immediate to a new and brighter future.

6

Leadership and Collaboration

———————

Courageousness: stepping into the void

A boat is safe in the harbour, but that's not what boats are for.
Maria Boulding, quoted in
Angela Ashwin, *Faith in the Fool*

> Once more unto the breach, dear friends, once more;
> Or close the wall up with our English dead.
> In peace there's nothing so becomes a man
> As modest stillness and humility:
> But when the blast of war blows in our ears,
> Then imitate the action of the tiger;
> Stiffen the sinews, summon up the blood.
> William Shakespeare, *Henry V*, Act III

It is tempting to begin this chapter with a heroic, out-of-the-ordinary story of courage – an act such as the clarion summoning of King Henry V as he musters his troops into the breach in Shakespeare's famous play. This is the dramatic courage of mountain climbing ilk, or survival in extreme conditions. All this is 'big courage' – inspirational as well as inescapable. But courage is also prosaic, wearisome and earthbound – the courage of a parent living with the terminal illness of their child, for instance. In the news this week 900 dockworkers in Portsmouth are faced with losing their jobs in the near future. Courage for them means dealing with an unclear future, living daily with the uncertainty of whether other employment will be found.

Every day our leadership can face the unknown, and cross the lines into unfamiliar territory. Clergy life requires us to journey outwards into situations both pastoral and practical, which needs courage and often seems like stepping into darkness because we have no previous experience and feel unequipped. The first time I took the funeral of a child was a case in point. Knowing the theory is one thing, but standing on the doorstep praying fervently, 'Lord, help me not to say anything inappropriate' was the reality. But as Maria Boulding suggests, our calling is not one of safety: our role as priest is a bravely prophetic one – we are asked to move out from the confines of the places where we feel safe, venturing into the agonies of the human heart, undertaking projects that not many others will take responsibility for. Throughout my own ministry, often in the context of a funeral, people ask me: 'How do you manage to do what you do?' – an awareness that absorbing pain and grief is a road that not many feel called to walk down because of its cogent effect upon us. John Lees, in his book *Secrets of Resilient People*, talks of courage in terms of pointing either *inwards* or *outwards*. We may need courage to challenge our inner demons at 2.00 a.m., as we beat down voices that feed our insecurities and uncertainties; we also need courage to deal with the things on the outside, like leading a congregation into a new stage in church life, challenging those we employ to be accountable, or being a prophetic voice even when we know it is likely to make us unpopular. Within solid and honest leadership lies a mixture of vulnerability, humility, and even a little appropriate arrogance in knowing that we are called (sometimes by default because of our role) to bring to birth a new vision or to grasp the proverbial bull by the horns.

The human tendency is to focus on acts of bravery that constitute 'wow factor' courage, and we often believe there is something wrong with us if we struggle to feel it. In *Prescription for Anxiety*, Leslie Weatherhead says this:

> We do not need a lecture on psychology to tell us that courage
> is not the virtue of those who do not know what fear is. I do

not believe there are such people. Courage is possessed by the person who estimates the fear-causing situation but summons all his resources and meets it.

Courage is strengthened by living daily a brave life when all we feel like doing is running and hiding. Courage is needed every time we enter a situation of extreme pastoral sensitivity; it is needed when we try to shift deep-seated opinions held by a community, when we sit alone in a darkened church knowing that human and financial resources are dwindling away and we are the ones who have to sort it. Like resilience, courage is woven into our very sinews.

The story of the apparently insignificant David – shepherd-boy and harp player – and the apparently insuperable giant – Goliath – from 1 Samuel 17 is well known. The scenario is this: the Israelites gather for battle in Socoh, a Judean town. They camp on one hill, facing the Philistine army who are on another hill, a deep valley between them. The text says that Goliath was a huge man – nearly 3 metres tall – and he presents himself when the time comes, wearing heavy armour and carrying a bronze javelin. Goliath shouts his challenge to the Israelites, and verse 17.11 tells us that even Saul was terrified. David arrives at the Israelite camp almost by default. His older brothers are part of Saul's army, and their father Jesse asks David to take food supplies to them to discover the state of play. Even before we get to the battle event, some interesting dynamics come into play in terms of courage. First, David is young and has clearly been kept at home because he is considered not strong enough to fight. He arrives just as Goliath is announcing his daily challenge like a broken record, searching out an Israelite combatant. But no one comes forward. Initially, David's courage emerges as he simply asks questions of his brothers: 'What shall be done for the man who kills this Philistine?' Mocked by his brothers and others he finally lands up in front of King Saul, who also questions his suitability for offering to fight. But he perseveres, using his courage to challenge the prejudice of others. Second, David uses his own experience as defender of his flock to persuade Saul that it should be he who tackles the giant. 'I regularly confront ferocious animals,' he says, 'so why should it not be me who takes on Goliath?' Saul gives David his own armour for protection, but this is discarded because David feels it is cumbersome to him. Instead he simply walks into the fray with what he knows – his shepherd's stick with sling and stones.

In other words, David's courage is represented only in the person that he is and the tools he comes with, even though his sling was probably more powerful than the boyish catapult popular myth sometimes suggests. But even knowing this, compared to Goliath, David seems at a great disadvantage. In this situation bravery and vulnerability are juxtaposed and David uses both to tackle a situation that no one previously has had the courage to grasp. Using his previous experience, just with the tools of his everyday existence, he becomes the leader of an army. Courage here is the taking of initiative when the odds seem stacked against him.

As David and Goliath confront one another David again steels himself against more taunting. Goliath jeers at David's apparently simple battle implement of shepherd's stick, as well as his smallness. But David has the mighty weapon of his God on his side – a God who does not need swords and spears to save people, in the words of 1 Samuel 17.47. After this, the action flows quickly. The text tells us that David runs forwards – he does not wait. Using the only tool that he knows – the sling and shot – he obliterates Goliath in one swift action. Here both inner and outer courage are played out magnificently. As the story continues we are told that David was successful in everything he did because, 'the LORD was with him' (1 Sam. 18.14).

In terms of courage this is the key. Courage in Christian leadership is about an understanding of our own psychological and human limitations and drawing on the power of God at every turn, and the strength of the Spirit both within and without us. The implications for clergy as courageous leaders include the following elements. Sometimes just asking the questions – naming the problems – becomes an act of courage, as it did for David. Courage also develops and grows, just as it did for this shepherd-boy, and while we can help ourselves by adding to our own skill base through additional training, ultimately we bring just our plain selves, with the experience and tools that we know into situations of challenge and difficulty. David drew on courage to overcome his own internal lack of confidence and the lack of belief others felt in him – a dynamic that younger clergy sometimes face from older members of a congregation.

John Lees talks about a further dimension, which lies in a courage *to* and a courage *from* concept; we can see this in the energy of this biblical story. David summons the courage to go into a situation using only the skills and tools he inherently has; he then uses his vulnerability to lead others into a situation of decisiveness when they are procrastinating and cowardly. It seems astonishing that in a 40-day period not one macho soldier was found willing to fight Goliath! In ministry this may manifest itself by our leadership taking on the representative role, the spokesperson, the individual who decides practically or theologically to move a situation forward, or change something that has become stuck. Courageousness means being the catalyst, the stimulus that accelerates decisions and allows subsequent progress to be made. My husband remembers calling a public meeting in a previous rural parish which had found itself at a point of crisis. He stood up to speak about the reality of having perhaps to close a church, but not one member of the PCC said anything to support his explanation even though in theory they were all behind him. As it turned out the result was a mustering of money and talents to renew that church for the future, but for a while he felt in a lonely place. Reordering projects can be another example of when courage is needed to take others forward. Often a congregation understands what needs to happen, and are in favour of alterations to a building or growth in ministry, but feel that they do not have the skills or authority to step into the breach to change what may have become a stagnant situation.

Authority goes hand in hand with courage, as it does for David, who speaks and behaves with much inner strength and composure. We might understand authority as when there is nothing we are scared of, when we gather the courage to face our fears, tying them up so that they do not unleash their pernicious power within us. Lees describes it like this: 'You know you want to get there, and you're half-ready to move, but it takes the kind of final deep-breath moment you need before diving into icy water.'

One of my childhood fears was walking over swampy ground, and to this day I dislike marshland and panic if I think my feet are going to sink into anything. But on Saturday mornings on TV, I watched with fascination Ron Ely as Tarzan who was always falling into quaggy jungle pits. But Tarzan (not the bad guys) always managed to get out of such predicaments. Our leadership requires this ability to 'get out' too – to move ourselves and others on. It plays itself out most powerfully as we find the courage to look within ourselves in repentance and also to forgive others. So often congregations and other groups get stuck in a place where the known, even when the situation is dire, feels safer and easier than change. Leading others out or away from, to be a facilitator of change continually, takes not only courage but energy of every kind.

I'm a bit of a fan of the TV reality show *I'm a Celebrity . . . Get Me Out of Here!* Celebrities agree to spend a few weeks camping in the Australian jungle, where they undergo a number of personal and group challenges. From the comfort of my insect-free living room I enjoy witnessing their courage as spiders are poured over their heads or they have to swim through snake-infested ponds. This might be pointless courage but those who participate often do not know until the last minute what their horrendous ordeal is going to be. There is a sense of them having to rise to the occasion, steeling themselves to endure, finding courage on a daily basis, *as they go along*. David did this too, delivering food and gathering news as he visited the battle site, and yet found himself the one facing Goliath. There is the sense, then, of us mustering the courage in situations where we have to think on our feet or step quickly into a void where it is impossible to know the outcome, as the famous words from *Henry V* suggest. Henry's men knew what they had to do – attack a gap in the wall of the city of Harfleur where the army was held under siege – but not what the outcome would be. Sometimes courage becomes about keeping our imaginations in check, guarding the doubts that slide unhelpfully into our minds, so that we do not allow the fear of what might never happen to incapacitate our natural bravery. Rowan Williams, in *Writing in the Dust*, quotes Simone Weil who says that the danger of imagination is that it fills up the void when what we need to learn is how to live in the *presence* of the void. Our courage is often found in the power cut as opposed to full daylight. Courage is about being able to take risks – sometimes difficult in a risk-averse society such as ours.

The 2012 film *Argo* is based on a true story – *The Master of Disguise* by Tony Mendez. It charts the escape of the six remaining American hostages who failed to get out from Iran in 1979 after the American embassy was stormed by activists. With dubious support from the US government, Mendez flies to Tehran with an elaborate plan to dupe the Iranian government. With fake Canadian passports the hostages take on the personae of members of a film crew, apparently in Iran to produce a science fantasy called 'Argo'. Each hostage memorizes a complete fake identity and the group manages to escape by the skin of their teeth as the authorities eventually discover the subterfuge. Mendez puts himself at huge risk by flying into a situation of danger, and it takes much courage for the hostages to take up this grave and risky challenge. Their courage is demonstrated in a situation in which people have simply found themselves by default – one of unpredictability and volatility.

More than anything, courage in leadership is about retaining and developing the inner energy to be a person who lovingly helps others progress. Courage sends out the message that however gigantic or insolvable the problem feels, there is always a way to move forwards even if it isn't the preferred choice of how we might implement change. Courage is about stating how things are, about naming the demons, speaking with compassion and truth into situations others find difficult to clarify or where the way ahead cannot be discerned. Courage is, using the image of a matador, about taking initiative in situations where we have nothing but our naked selves with which to grasp the bull by the horns. As the church faces a period of potentially gargantuan yet creative change, our leadership must be filled with courage, rooted in the strength of a greater power who transforms our trembling attempts to herald in a new era.

Graciousness: the uncompetitive edge

> Never before have we been so aware of the interconnectedness of the choices our leaders make.
>
> Simon Walker, *The Undefended Leader*

Kinky Boots is a film comedy from 2005 based on the true story of a failing Northamptonshire shoe factory. After his father's death, Charlie Price takes over a business that makes classic handcrafted shoes. For several years the factory has faced stiff competition from cheap Polish imports and Charlie is confronted with the task of laying off longstanding staff. He ventures to London for inspiration, where he inadvertently meets a drag queen, Lola. He ends up watching her show, and Lola points out that the boots drag queens wear are often made for women and therefore are not strong enough to take the weight of a typical man. This proves a lightbulb moment for Charlie, as he realizes that his business could reinvent itself to provide a niche market for fetish footwear. He returns to Northampton with renewed vision, and with Lola's help persuades his staff to make the turn-around. After being exposed on the high fashion catwalks of Milan the product is a unanimous success. Throughout, Charlie feels the weight of responsibility he has for his staff. There is a pivotal moment in the film when not only does he need to persuade others to share the new vision, he needs them to embrace it as well. Initially, this proves a tall order for the conservative workers of this traditional factory, but it comes about because Charlie shows his own vulnerability at a point when he understands that he can't 'go it alone' any more.

Some of these dynamics might seem familiar to clergy leading in an increasingly eclectic environment. We present our faith in traditional, often 'classic' forms through liturgy and preaching, sometimes trying to ignore the spectre of the more vibrant and successful parish next door, which attracts more youth, ups its numbers or does ministry more inventively than we do. Leadership, as Charlie finds in *Kinky Boots*, at times makes us feel alarmingly alone, under pressure to be something we feel we cannot be. During my own ministry I have had moments when I have smugly announced the success of the vivacious initiative I am currently part of, but also others where I gnash my proverbial teeth underneath a spirit of collegiality, feeling hotly jealous of others' achievements. I am sure I am not alone in such honest admissions. We are not meant to be competitive as clergy, yet there are times we feel these pressures quite acutely. But it should not be so bleak, as we remember that church life is and always should be about working with others, sharing the strains and stresses. The criterion of 'leadership and collaboration' states the following skills in terms of knowledge and disposition: 'Any potential leader must have an awareness of issues concerning responsibility and power, particularly in relation to group dynamics and expressed in a servant and team ministry.' Authority must be used to recognize and encourage the gifts of others; 'Individuals need to be able to exercise effective collaborative leadership as part of a team in order to release and enable others to fulfil their calling to ministry and mission.'

If we feel capable, it is sometimes easier to get on with projects ourselves rather than trying to lead others, because this saves time and energy. But if this forms the majority of our working practice then we will soon find ourselves in a lonely place. The idea of graciousness sounds perhaps like old-fashioned 'gentility' but I believe it is an underrated quality that needs to be reinvented. Graciousness is more than being gently benign; it is potentially something more robust. Graciousness suggests allowing something or someone to take the forefront, our potential stepping aside in order to enable someone else to speak or act, however we might be feeling. This is a conscious, deliberate and *active* idea and asks that our leadership puts the voices and ministries of others before our (sometimes) stronger or more adamant vision. It is a quality that admits that others might have more experience or expertise than we do, might see something we don't, or might just be right when we are steadily barking up the wrong tree. Graciousness presents a patient response when confronted with injustice or unfair treatment, seeking to understand the other's point of view while sitting on our own innate sense of injury. Properly put into practice, graciousness can take on a radical and counter-cultural expression of loving courtesy which is Christ-like in its intentions. More than anything, graciousness moves us away from the competitiveness that potentially limits the spaciousness of our soul's generosity of spirit.

Right from the outset, Jesus formed a circle of supportive workers around him to translate and implement the vision for the kingdom of God. This vision grew to become understood as a collective and collaborative one. From the very beginning he was clear that his sole personhood and ministry would not be able to fulfil every expectation. The sending out of the disciples in Mark 6 is the only place in the Gospels where it states unequivocally that the men venture out *in pairs*. The disciples are given power and authority to do ministry that is significant and cogent – healing the sick and driving out demons. Working in pairs meant having some form of emotional and physical protection – shielded (at least a little) from harsh reactions and being bullied by those who might seek to take advantage of them. The disciples are stronger together for the sake of the gospel – the work of evangelizing and persuading is lonely and demanding alone. Being in pairs also means that any success or glory can be shared too, in terms of successful healing and conversion – an anti-primadonna tactic on Jesus' part perhaps? The disciples are explicitly told not to take provisions or home comforts with them, not even the essentials; they are to go out in a state of complete vulnerability – they are equipped with only the clothes on their backs and the authority given them by Jesus. Part of their ministry, then, is to offer both of these to those they find themselves among, and to accept the hospitality of strangers. But in spite of these supposed disadvantages, the disciples are successful in their travels through the land, healing and preaching the Good News – together.

The disciples have obviously arrived at a point where Jesus feels confident enough to send them out in his name, and this is perhaps extraordinary for men who were, to all intents and purposes, unrefined fishermen. In his book *Leading Out of Who You Are: Discovering the Secrets of Undefended Leadership*, Simon Walker cites leaders possessing similar granted authority who are set apart because of a characteristic of 'undefendedness'. These are people, he says, who have often experienced personal sacrifice, struggle and loss, who are characters who have been tested and refined in an ongoing process. The disciples perhaps were 'undefended' men such as this – people who gave up much, entered the steep learning curve of a conversion experience and changed their lifestyles from settled to itinerant. Clergy, through the process of formation, enter into a similar active process. In their case this results in them becoming people who potentially develop into stronger, more uninhibited leaders who are 'liberated from the need to dominate, to conquer and oppress, to consume, to acquire . . . because they are free within themselves'. This seems to be a perfect base for collaborative ministry. We believe in the moral authority that we have as we move outwards and onwards without fear and in freedom, desiring and searching for others with whom to share the task.

Collaborative leaders need to model graciousness for a number of reasons. Most of us know people within our congregations who hold on tightly to a specific role or task, often finding it difficult to step down so that another person can grow into the role or take up the challenge. The satisfying of their own deep desire to feel valued or needed often obstructs the empowerment of others. But this is ultimately not healthy, either for the individual concerned or for church life. Our focus, as consecrated men and women, is to make available all of our skills for the good of the church and community life. It is vital that we practise the ministry we find particularly fulfilling, but as leaders we sometimes have to give up activities we love if it means the new authorization and skilling of others. Graciousness is about remembering that as priests we are always called to be servants first and leaders second.

According to Simon Walker, the primary goal of leadership is to empower and enable others to take responsibility. This is surely what Jesus does, and Paul too, in the establishment of the message of the kingdom and the early Church communities. At the feeding of the 5,000, Jesus challenges the disciples to sort out the problem of the people's hunger themselves. Those of us in leadership positions can get tired of the 'dumping' that happens to us at times – the phone call that informs us of a specific situation we don't know how to act on, the suggestion of a new project, the arrival of a 'problem' that no one else can sort. Our task, as people called to work together with other Christians, is not to bury our heads in the sand but rather to say, 'Let's work together', and to ask, 'Who is with me?' as well as to state 'I will play my part'. We are called to serve, courageously and vulnerably, while allowing and encouraging others to take responsibility as well. Walker suggests that collaboration is about enabling people to step out of passivity; right leadership can be a way of helping them to grow up and away from false understandings of the clergy doing everything. In collaborative ministry graciousness is an inner attitude that stems from a place of deep self-assuredness and security – a more ideal than real place, for many of us. We consciously compare ourselves with others who we believe to be more talented, more energetic, more theologically able than ourselves. Yet clergy are extractors and propagators of an ever-refreshed view of God's kingdom. Graciousness is about us always remembering that we should be free and generous with our skills, sharing them so that they become tools that can enable others to flourish and take off as well.

Someone once described the Church as a 'flat' organization – a term I chewed over for weeks. At the time I was struggling with a sense of inner restlessness. Never describing myself as ambitious, I nevertheless found myself in a place where I realized that I was experiencing the yearning to stretch my wings, enjoy a new challenge in some new form. The term 'flat' was being used to refer to an organization that has a limited career ladder – and it cannot be denied that there is a hierarchy inherent in the Church of England and its episcopal structures. So ambition in terms of being competitive for 'status' jobs does not seem a helpful or healthy option for the average clergy person. Rather we need to provide opportunities to rediscover self-worth, to develop new skills, as well as enjoying the challenge of new responsibilities. All these things need an environment that encourages a holy exploration through open conversation and transparency with those who take responsibility for ministerial reviews and ever-shifting posts. Clergy should not be embarrassed about wanting new challenges; ours is a professional job that draws the most talented of people, many of whom have a huge skill and quality set. With this should be a renewed championing of others and the acknowledgement of the fact that there is no future for us as clergy leaders if we insist on going it alone, walking over others in the process.

Many churches struggle to pay their parish share, so the reality is that with rapidly decreasing funds we will have no choice but to work together and join with others as 'church'. The parish system no longer has much significance in some areas, but in others it is healthily evolving because of new and emerging needs within a community. At a recent chapter meeting, a colleague in a parish with a different church tradition from my own spoke about every church developing its own area of specialism. In his church he has struggled to bring in even a relatively commonplace all-age service; in his parish almost every service is from the Prayer Book and east-facing. We joked as I mentioned that a few of my parishioners would happily come to his services on the occasions when our church is noisy from children's laughter. Of course, there are dangers here of making church a subjective business, where we fail to challenge our folk to develop a tolerance and love for 'the other'.

But there is something of a point to be made. All leaders have to do a certain amount of run-of-the-mill ministry, but most of us exhaust ourselves with far too much. It might be better perhaps to think carefully about what we could offer in terms of what is really needed in a particular place – where the gaps are – as well as where gifts and skills lie in the resources of our own folk that can be developed. In a recent article in the *Church Times*, Stephen Spencer suggests a return to monastic approaches for models of collaborative ministry and clergy-working patterns for the future. Over the centuries the

Church has enjoyed a variety of organizational formats – from 'a priest in every parish' to the parochial system, to voluntary associations and friendship groups set up for the benefit of its members. In his own town Spencer notes that there are nine centres of worship, all seeking to serve the town as a whole with distinctive ministry. Their changing (yet ancient) function is one of oversight and development – encouraging and co-coordinating the ministry that their congregations undertake. Such ministry is both what is specifically stimulated by the Church and the things Christian people just 'do' in other networks and environments. Spencer concludes: 'Fewer priests are needed, but they should be priests who know how to facilitate the ministry of others. It does, however, call on all churches to work in co-operation with one another, so that they may address as many local needs as possible.' In the context of this discussion then, our call to collaboration should extend not just to those we work with within our own four walls but outwards towards a potential new ecumenism as well.

Some years ago I walked up Mount Kinabalu in Borneo with my husband. The 14,000-foot trek took two days – hard physical effort, climbing uphill through steamy heat and semi-jungle. The path was distinct and at a pinch we could probably have 'gone it alone'. Two Australian lads raced on ahead, trying to prove their masculine prowess, but then were too exhausted to walk the final leg on the second day. However, the camaraderie of the rest of our small group produced significant encouragement when the going got tough, and the medical expertise of our local guide was vital when altitude sickness crept up on us all. Climbing the mountain remains to this day a significant physical achievement for me, and my guess is that it does for the others too. There are times when it feels spiritually and humanly apt to celebrate our individual successes because leadership requires us to step out on our own or to do something no one else could in a particular context. But on the whole we do things better when we seek the advice, expertise and perspective of others, as exemplified in the ultimate model we have of the God we believe in who is relational, Trinitarian and deeply inter-connected with all of humanity: a God who encourages and enables us to achieve great things together.

7

Relationships

———•·•·•———

Adaptability: clergy as flexible friend

It is not the strongest or the most intelligent who will survive
but those who can best manage risk.   Charles Darwin

In your service of others you will feel, you will care, you will
hurt, you will have your heart broken.   Michael Ramsey

The Cu Chi tunnels are an elaborate network of underground
passageways situated approximately 40 kilometres north-west
of Ho Chi Minh City, Vietnam. Constructed initially during
the 1940s, these tunnels were further developed during the
Vietnam War and used as a hideout for Vietcong soldiers who
lived in them, some surviving for many years. The passages
gave them a defensive advantage over the American soldiers
who found it difficult to locate the network's entry points
because of camouflage on the ground. The Cu Chi community ate, slept and planned attacks there; children were born
and marriages solemnized. Their construction was ingenious –
bamboo pipes were used as air channels, concealed in anthills
above ground.

The ability of human beings to adapt to a multiplicity of
circumstances and potential crises has been understood since
Darwin named the process of evolution. It could be argued,
perhaps, that in no other profession does the ability to adapt
manifest itself quite as evidently as in the clergy. In today's
Church, external tasks demand unremitting multi-skilling, while
the internal roller-coaster resulting from absorbing others'

emotions can be stimulating as well as draining. Adaptability is vital.

A couple of months ago I noted how two days in my week had panned out.

The first day began with taking an assembly at a local primary school, where I had to be outwardly extrovert, 'out there' attempting to relate the theme of endings (it being the end of the school year) with the Ascension to children aged between four and ten. After this I visited a new parishioner in his home. There were no curtains at the windows and no carpet on the floor, and he had a small child. I left feeling that I wanted to help him out, yet also energized because he is an artist of extraordinary talent. I then headed to our local crematorium where I conducted the funeral for a man where the only mourners were the funeral directors. The evening was spent leading a monthly class we run in our parish for parents bringing their children for baptism. The following day was equally varied. I found myself at short notice being interviewed by a newspaper reporter from the *Independent* about the food bank project we run from one of our churches, then passed the rest of the morning with two parishioners having coffee (both of whose husbands are bankers). In the afternoon I spent some time supervising a Reader in training, followed by an agonizing hour and a half with the parents of a middle-aged man who had just taken his own life. By the end of the second day I was beginning to seriously look forward to my day off.

The description of these two days will resonate with many clergy – it is fairly typical of the variety and unpredictability of how ministry takes shape. There are some 'givens' – tasks that we find easy because we have done them a thousand times before – but other situations take us by surprise, and many need gentle and sensitive handling. After these two days I reflected on how much my outer as well as my inner life had ebbed and flowed, how I intuitively adapted myself around the variety of physical, social and emotional situations I found myself a part of. Unpacked, this is what it looked like in terms of the skills needed, as well as some of the accompanying feelings. On day one: ability to connect with children (assembly); ability to communicate enthusiasm to a new person and their gifts (visit to new parishioner); ability to bring dignity to a sad situation (funeral without family mourners and deal with my inner anguish within it); ability to communicate a warmth of welcome and the delight in new parents' joy (baptism preparation session). On day two: ability to respond quickly and be able to communicate a story so that the press would print it in a reasonable way (impromptu *Independent* interview); ability to talk about yoga and children and other subjects familiar to ladies of leisure (communicating with wealthy parishioners); ability to be a genuine 'critical friend' (time with trainee Reader); ability to give some support in a situation of intense desolation, and not come out with insensitive or flippant religious platitudes (funeral visit). The emotions that accompany this churning turbulent itinerary are as follows: energized, exhausted, anxiety, deep sadness, joy, surprise, jealousy; deep sadness (again) and empathy. We need the ability not just to wear different hats externally, but to manage the hidden results that no one except God and those closest to us ever see.

Clergy, from the very beginning, tend to be adaptable. Often switching from a previous life and career, they are taken apart on their formation journey and slowly (and hopefully sensitively) put back together through theological training. During one lifetime of service, the places and communities we find ourselves in will require different approaches and strategies, as Paul understood very clearly in the centres where he established the faith. Although there may be something of a structure to our week, potentially every clergy day is different. My guess is that most of us have personality types that enjoy this variety, but it requires a chameleon-like adaptability to continually deal with the expansive range of tasks, pastoral needs and tangled theological questions encountered on a day-to-day basis. We become the catcher of issues that fall through others' nets, the default option; we become the person on whom people dump their unresolved issues, purely because there is sometimes no other professional to plug the gaps. Adaptability means dealing with the range of human emotions that others need help to cope with, often at times of significant 'rites of passage'. It means adapting when faced with the unexpected, swiftly thinking ourselves into situations of stress and crisis.

But adaptability is about continuously allowing our ego to slip away and intuitively empathizing with the joys and tribulations of others, responding to the pastoral needs of others. It is about carrying within us a hospitable and humble space that genuinely wants to relate and serve. Vanessa Herrick and Ivan Mann, in their book reflecting on vulnerability in leadership, *Jesus Wept*, talk about our accepting 'the contradictory forces within and without . . . a decision to be with Christ wherever he is and wherever he wants us to be at a particular place and time'. Similarly Henri Nouwen speaks in *The Wounded Healer* on the dangers of aloofness – the cold opposite of adaptability – as it refuses to enter into the reality of a situation, protecting the heart of the priest as 'professional', squashing the desire to empathize or to share in someone's life.

In Cambodia many communities live and work on Tonle Sap, the largest freshwater lake in south-east Asia, which covers nearly one-seventh of the country's landmass during monsoon season. Many of the homes and business are built on rafts, which can move with the changing volume of water. There is a floating school, supermarket, pagoda and church. I love the idea of the floating church in particular, which moves to adapt to external conditions so that it remains intact and never gets swamped. The ability to be taken in one direction for a particular reason at a certain time but then draw away again is a powerful model of adaptability. As leaders we allow ourselves to be gently taken, conveyed backwards and forwards by the activity of God's Spirit, even when we might feel out of our depth, vulnerably aware that at times our human presence is actually sufficient. Encouraging such fluidity in a congregation as a whole is also an interesting concept. Adaptability is about the need for a paradigm shift, a new understanding of who we are as Church, along with self-awareness that we must adapt with the times rather than remain a static institution.

Many characters in the Bible model adaptability, but Abraham is one whose heterogeneous life provides a strong example. Abraham's narrative begins when he is already old; the text says 75 but that is probably a symbolic age. His age is interesting in itself, as we sometimes complain that older people find it difficult, even impossible, to change how they live or the way they do things. Abraham's life spans chapters 12 through to 25 of Genesis. He is of stoical character but clearly has an inner ability to go with the flow, to adapt to the new challenges that God asks of him. God asks Abram (as he is at the beginning) to leave his native country, and he commences a journey that takes him through many new lands. In a tribal-centred culture, God asks him to be the father of a new race that will be distinctively different. A famine forces his entourage back to Egypt, where Abram pretends to the king that Sarah is his sister, not his wife, and has to face the king's wrath when he realizes he has been deceived. In Chapter 13, Abram moves onwards again, this time to Mamre. Once settled in this new place he hears that his nephew Lot has been captured by warring armies; duty-bound, he sets out to restore Lot's lands to him once again. In chapter 16 Abram deals with internal struggles – a resentful, upset wife and a taunting concubine. By chapter 17, years have passed and Abram is 99 years old; it is here that his name is changed to Abraham, as God promises again the covenant of an allocated land, and many descendants. Abraham demonstrates his loyalty and allegiance by promising that every eight-day-old male child will be circumcised. Chapter 18 describes the hospitality he shows to 'angels' and then Abraham suddenly finds himself in something of a crisis situation; he becomes advocate, pleading for the protection of the city of Sodom, a wicked and almost irredeemable place in the eyes of God. In chapter 21 Abraham copes with the sadness of sending Hagar and Ishmael away because of Sarah's jealousy, and in chapter 22 he faces the ultimate testing from God, who asks him to sacrifice his own son. The final chapters see Abraham mourning the death of Sarah, but then he takes another wife, Keturah, a marriage that brings further descendants.

In his one life, this great man is staggeringly stretched by God. He adapts to travelling ever onwards into unknown territory; he wrestles with warring tribes and a host of awkward characters. He is asked to leave his native land; he deals with famine and the internal struggles of his family. His own identity is changed, as is his name, but through it all he tries to listen to where God is leading him next. He shows hospitality to strangers, becomes an advocate for the innocent, is faced with the possibility of committing infanticide, and then with bereavement. All this indicates a highly adaptable human being, living a life that also incorporates the already discussed idea of resilience.

One of my favourite films is *Grow Your Own*, the story of some keen northern allotment-holders who are forced to share their green space with a small group of traumatized asylum-seekers. The film is about the gradual knitting together of these two groups, after initial, but perhaps understandable, ignorance and prejudice. Some of the original gardeners are happy to adapt their 'space' to include these new folk while others remain stoically unable to do so until the end. The film demonstrates the pain that adapting to a radically new environment or group of people can bring – for both the allotment-holders and the asylum-seekers. One of the most touching aspects of the film emerges in the healing that happens as the original gardeners allow themselves (and their 'policies') to be changed by their encounters with their internally damaged new neighbours. Genuinely adapting, then, is about us changing inside. Because clergy do this continuously it often feels like a way of life – a costly yet rewarding one: costly in that it is exhausting to experience the range of emotions both in others and within ourselves, often within a short space of time, and rewarding because we make sincere connections with others, often at significant moments in their lives. With this comes the establishing of relationships, leading to community connections and sometimes the beginning of a journey of faith.

Being adaptable does not mean that we should be in any way insincere. Like our increasingly multipurpose buildings, it is more about providing those we encounter with the possibility of connecting with God through a multiplicity of experiences. These days we need our buildings to be flexible too. A few years ago I visited the Bromley by Bow Healthy Living Centre, established in 1984 by the newly arrived United Reformed minister Andrew Mawson. This visionary leader, experiencing a dwindling and ageing congregation, understood that the church would have to drastically adapt its understanding of what it means to be Church if it wanted to become a hub, alive with the life of God. This has now been achieved: the place is a vibrant community centre of energy and spirituality, encompassing a health centre, community café and garden and local nursery. Situated in a multicultural area, a whole variety of religious festivals are celebrated in the centre, enabling barriers of prejudice to be broken down. The centre uses the arts to help build self-esteem and its various programmes encourage those with mental and physical disabilities to be creative. The website says that the centre is 'responsive to the needs of the community and uses the buildings and facilities in imaginative and resourceful ways. The interior of the Church was redesigned to suit its many uses.'

Jesus himself was infinitely adaptable, particularly in communicating the message of the kingdom, depending on who he was speaking too. His message differed in style and approach, adapting to whether he was dialoguing with individuals or addressing large groups, whether he was challenging the religious leaders of the day or trying to get his inner core of disciples to understand the message they sometimes considered obscure. He was teacher, preacher, prophet, consoler, healer, friend and scapegoat, among many other things. Last year, as part of a town-wide appeal at Harvest time, we supported ShelterBox, an international charity that provides relief to communities who have suffered environmental and humanitarian disasters. Each box contains what is necessary to survive in a particular emergency situation: a substantial tent, a portable stove and utensils, blankets, and drawing materials for children are included. Boxes are adapted depending on the crisis, while the box itself can be used as a table, a bath or storage facility, its 'space' admirably adaptable to fit the needs of those it serves, maximizing its potential to genuinely help people to feel human after experiencing trauma. Within our iconic personhood as priest, we too carry the possibility and ability to be such a 'kingdom thing' for those we celebrate with and help heal, in whatever situation we find ourselves.

Cherishing: the long, loving look

The question for the church of the future is not 'Have I provided dogmatic information sufficient for salvation?' but rather, 'Have I shown compassion to those who need it and the love of God to those denied it?'

Robin R. Meyers, *Saving Jesus from the Church*

You are as prone to love, as the sun is to shine; it being the most delightful and natural employment of the soul of man: without which you are dark and miserable.

Thomas Traherne, *Centuries*

S21 is the notorious prison located in the middle of Phnom Penh, Cambodia. It was used during the atrocities committed by the Khmer Rouge, and was the place where hundreds of people of intelligence and sensitivity were brought to be incarcerated and tortured before they were herded out to be murdered in the 'killing fields'. Now a national museum, visitors are allowed to wander through the buildings containing the former cells. It's a place where one can imagine the anguish of what happened there, the screams compressed into its bloodstained walls. It is a chilling reminder of the capacity of unadulterated human evil. After I visited this place, its macabre overtones resulted in a sleepless night, as it hit home that when this gruesome place was in operation in the late 1970s I was enjoying a secure and happy childhood.

For those of us who claim to believe in a God of love it's crucial that at some point on our faith journey we wrestle with the problem of the evil and the agony it produces. 'Why is there so much suffering and pain when we believe in a God of love?' remains one of the most challenging questions about human existence that people continually ask our leadership. Intellectually we know the answer: God shares our pain; suffering is often more about what human beings do to one another than how God does or doesn't respond. It's about a divine love that refuses to be confined within a system of predictable expectations or punishments. But that said, people can still find it immeasurably difficult to believe sincerely in a God who loves and cares for us when there seems no evident intervention during times of intense global hell. Or when your child dies from cancer.

Sitting underneath one of the fragrant frangipani trees (these trees symbolize appropriately 'broken hearts' in this part of the East) in the grounds of S21 was a survivor of the Khmer Rouge, now in his seventies. He was selling a book that told his story. An engineer, and therefore 'useful' to the prison authorities, he had been kept alive. I marvelled at his presence here – if it was me, I thought, this terrible prison would be the last place on earth I would want to return to. I talked to him briefly. A person of immense gentleness, he felt that it was now his responsibility to educate others about the history of what had happened there.

I'm either oversensitive or an amateur mystic, but at times I feel overwhelmed by the pain of the world. On a rare Sunday when I was sitting in the pew, I looked around at people seated near me. It seems that all of them carried a story of heartbreak – bereavement, loneliness, or unsolvable problems. Jesus the Good Shepherd says, in John 10.14, that he knows his sheep. Being included in a church community means that over time we get to know those who come through the doors, with their issues of hurt and brittleness. Leadership gives us this special privilege too. It is a powerful experience to be known, understood and accepted, because it is only then that we can truly feel loved. Most of us will only stay in a church if we feel loved and supported, even at a minimal level. Even as leaders, while we do all the usual ministry – mission initiatives, reordering buildings and running discipleship courses – essentially we too need to feel included and valued; we ourselves come with a yearning to be healed and to be soothed when we feel raw or unwanted. The God we believe in views every single human being as precious and important – every person in the history of the world's existence. Someone said to me recently that they were attracted to being part of the Church because they yearned to be 'somewhere that I mattered'. This is the beginning of cherish.

The word cherish takes love one step further, to someone or something we value highly. Cherish is a word we use in the vows of the wedding service. Cherish means treasuring another person; it means keeping a sense of the sacredness of one another, whoever they are. Cherish would mean that what took place at S21 might never happen again, if we worked at looking at each other like this for long enough: the long, loving look – how we believe God looks at us. Christians talk about love a lot; we bandy around the idea that God loves us all, but if we don't feel very loved ourselves then it can be a hard concept to grasp. Many of us struggle to understand how to love a God who can feel like an abstract or historical concept or both. Cherishing makes our love more distinctive by stretching it out more expansively to include those who might not get that much of it, or who may frankly not be very lovable. Cherish is about us using our energy intentionally and specifically in an effort to love others and to regard them as precious and unique.

The 1987 Danish film *Babette's Feast* is a study on the nature of love and how we choose to express it. In nineteenth-century Denmark two sisters live in an isolated village with their father, a highly regarded pastor of a small Protestant sect. A French refugee – Babette – is welcomed into the household where she serves the family as a servant. After the death of the pastor, Babette unexpectedly discovers that she has won a great deal of money through the lottery. She chooses to spend her entire fortune on an extravagant feast for the two sisters and their guests, commemorating the 100th year of their father's birth. Wendy Wright in *The Journal of Religion and Film* reflects on how many of the scenes in the film invite the viewer into a kind of 'long, loving look'; perhaps especially in those of the feast itself, which is portrayed with almost eucharistic sacramentalism. The scenes of the feast are presented like iconic stills where we are invited to view the humanity portrayed there with an almost devotional love and reverence, to contemplate the gentleness and preciousness within each individual person, however quirky or eccentric. We see through the characters into their souls, becoming aware of something infinitely rich and layered, as opposed to just a group of people eating a meal.

A story of the 'long and loving look' lived out in an earthed, practical situation comes from my own parish – an example of how we choose to look at others. Nikki is often at home with her small daughter. Where she lives, door-to-door salesmen (often ex-offenders) commonly come round selling things we don't need at over-inflated prices. Many people consider such folk an annoyance. One such man knocked on Nikki's door one morning. Rather than shutting the door in his face, she not only bought several things but sat him down and talked to him, one human being to another, displaying her natural graciousness. She had thought herself into this person's situation and felt she wanted to try to treat him kindly. The man's words to Nikki as he finally left her doorstep were, 'You are the only person on this estate who has given me any time and treated me with respect.' Cherishing even for 15 minutes changes the dynamic of someone's day; people don't forget this kind of love. Cherishing provides a potent antidote to the expansive pain of the world, which sometimes crushes our hearts with its vastness.

The Bible has many references to the fact that people are important to God: individuals, nations, people who are known, those who aren't known at all. Isaiah 43 describes Israel as precious and honoured in the sight of God because God loves his people. In Matthew 10 Jesus tells his followers not to be afraid because they are precious beyond measure, more than the tiny sparrows that God also loves. Our responsibility as Christian leaders means that we are called to cherish those who come into our churches and into our lives at any point, needing to be loved – just as throughout the Gospels Jesus cherished those with whom he had no prior relationship, time and time again. He scooped people up, sat them down and made them feel like they mattered – whether they were those he knew or anonymous individuals who were a temporary presence in his life.

Leaders are bound up with a thousand complex and intertwined relationships, in which a great deal is often invested. As clergy running an organization, we weigh up and assess folk all the time. Within our relationships we need to be diplomatic at the same time as being able to take a strong and decisive lead, regardless of others' equally strident opinions or apparent expertise. If we are painfully honest, at a time of dwindling resources when we desperately look out for people with money, skills and availability, it can sometimes be hard to love and give time to those we know will be of no practical or financial use to us as leaders. Similarly it can feel costly to cherish those who just waste our time for one reason or another – the 'black holes' of pastoral ministry – or those who promise much but never deliver. The criterion explored in this chapter looks at whether there is stability within ordinands' personal relationships, whether they are likely to be good people managers with the ability to get on with others, or whether they will upset and offend more than will be healthy and stable for the communities they are to serve. If we are good and intuitive leaders we are aware of this, but it is a costly thing for us always to be genuinely caring, to look at people as we believe God does, when we can be pushed for time or when people irritate and annoy us for various reasons, sometimes just simply clashing with our own personalities.

We need to model 'cherish' even more within the relationships we find ourselves involved in, because we are people whom others look to. Cherish marks out Church as a distinctive community that communicates the message that everyone reflects the beauty of God; it tells us that love can be found in people and places where it might have been expected to have disappeared long ago. Cherish is vital as a sign in a world where people are easily forgotten and horrendously dispensed with. Cherish provides a radically alternative way of looking at another human being – as awesome and wanted, in a world where employees are let go of casually because of temporary work contracts, where people are killed using biological weapons.

The story of the prodigal son in Luke 15 is a biblical example of how cherishing can be physically lived out. The father clearly knows and loves his younger son prior to his greedy squandering, but when this son comes to terms with his own estrangement, no conditions are stipulated by the father for his return. As he staggers home in his rock-bottom state, his father rushes out to envelop his son in his utter brokenness, seeing only future possibility; in doing so he transforms this moment into a new beginning. Cherish brings potential healing simply by the way we look at and treat others, our attitude towards them. Verse 20 says, 'But while he was still far off, his father saw him' – an interesting phrase to include. Within many of us we carry a sense of lostness, a searching for 'home' that will satisfy our deep emotional discontent, because home seems a long way away. What is needed is a sign of welcome, inclusion, warmth – an experience that tells us we are valued, necessary for a community, that we can be a part of it again, if we, like the lost son, have drifted away. Cherish can provide a powerful model for occasions in church life when relationships break down or need to be challenged, as happened in this story. Cherishing means the serious attempt to reconcile and resolve while keeping emotional and moral sensitivities always in mind.

In 2010 the Chinese artist Ai Weiwei's 'Sunflower Seeds' was the installation in the Turbine Hall in Tate Modern. An infinite grey sea was produced by 100 million seeds on the floor. At first glance all the seeds looked exactly the same, but in fact every single one had been hand-crafted from porcelain and painted individually in small workshops in the city of Jingdezhen. China is known for its mass production of cheap goods (mostly for the West) and intensive human labour. Through this work, the artist made subversive statements about the importance and cherishing of every human person and how bad work practices and damaging ideologies dehumanize people. Juliet Bingham, curator at Tate Modern, said: 'The precious nature of the material, the effort of production, the narrative and personal content create a powerful commentary on the human condition.' The work posed challenging questions, like, 'What does it mean to be an individual in today's society?' Ai Weiwei was recently named as the most powerful dissident in the art world. He was arrested because of the implications his work stimulates in a country where freedom of speech and artistic expression are still censored by a communist state.

The quotation from Thomas Traherne at the beginning of this section continues:

Objects without love are the delusion of life. The objects of love are its greatest treasures and without love it is impossible they should be treasures . . . to love all persons in all ages, all angels, all worlds, is divine and heavenly. Now you may see what it is to be a son of God more clearly.

To cherish and treasure those within our pastoral charge is sometimes difficult to get right in terms of balance. We must not offer a cloying 'loviness', we should not love with favouritism or agendas, and we should love indiscriminately – both those who contribute much with their talents and those who offer nothing but their pained selves. Our relational leadership should love with our heads and our hearts, with naturalness and with integrity, and with all of this we should accept the limitations of our own emotional capacity and cherish our souls' needs too. Cherish is not to be understood as a syrupy emotionalism but as a robust and prophetic looking that illuminates to the world that every human person is made in the image of God.

8

Personality

-•◆•-

Naturalness: no added sugar

A person must be converted twice; once from the natural to the
spiritual, and then again from the spiritual to the natural.

Eberhard Arnold

To be yourself in a world that is constantly trying to make you
something else is the greatest accomplishment.

Ralph Waldo Emerson

There's a shop my teenage daughter is particularly fond of.
Hollister sells a brand of clothing modelled on the fashionable,
laid-back surfing and outdoor lifestyle of California. During
the holidays, I went into our nearest store. The shop, decked
out with a fusion of styles from old-colonial to beach shack,
works. Pumping contemporary music along with large screens
of surfers on sun-streaked beaches is all part of its marketing
strategy. But it was the assistants that fascinated me most. All
were young (in their twenties or younger), slim and enviously
beautiful. I suddenly felt my age. One young man, bearing
an uncanny resemblance to a real-life Action Man, greeted me
with a 'Howyoudoing?' as we walked into the shop. Of course,
Hollister (linked with the Abercrombie and Fitch empire) has
done its research. It unashamedly knows its market and projects
an image that will sell its clothes at high prices. Promoting
the idea of eternal youth in such an artificial way made me feel
uncomfortable, as it dawned on me that all this was far from
'natural'. It is what it is, but as I was leaving I contemplated how

the shop potentially becomes oppressive to all who cannot live up to such an image themselves, perhaps particularly the young.

But 'natural', and the construction of this, has ironically become a sought-after commodity in Western society, perhaps because simply being human has become so much more complicated. The advertisements for Dove cosmetic products cleverly use natural beauty as a selling point, as they make a conscious effort to feature woman of all ages. Food that is organic and untampered with has given rise to artisan and farmers' markets in many towns throughout the country. Naturalness is big news, but what does it really mean? Sincerity, authenticity, a measure of unselfconsciousness are appealing; most of us usually warm to people who actually enjoy being themselves. Those we encounter as clergy, however, often experience a deep dissatisfaction because they are not essentially happy with who they are, trying continually to shape their character or physical appearance into someone they will never be.

For those of us with roles in vocational discernment there is a tightrope to be walked – that of developing confidence and new skills in someone who feels unworthy of their potential new role as a leader, while at the same time encouraging them to celebrate who they are. Every candidate for ministry also needs to fit into the framework of the traditional role of priest – the ontological and the functional – being and doing. These days vocation emerges at many stages of life. The crucial thing is that as the discernment process develops, a person's natural personality is challenged when necessary (should it be detrimental to ministerial practice and relationships), but never squashed, so that emerging leaders understand that God will work through the cracks and chinks of who they naturally are – always.

The criterion of Personality helps ordinands dig deep to explore who they are as individual people and to test whether they have an appropriate degree of self-awareness and self-acceptance to help them understand their own strengths and weaknesses in the rigours of ministry. Personality is a slippery concept – we know that we are uniquely loved by God and valued just as we are, although in reality we often find this hard to believe. There should be a stability and balance in terms of self-knowledge in addition to an open willingness to change and learn from weaknesses within our characters. There is also the strong strand in theological thinking that tells us that we need to leave the self behind. A prayer from Pierre Teilhard de Chardin encapsulates this tension: 'Lord, enfold me in the depths of your heart; and there, hold me, refine, purge, and set me on fire, raise me aloft, until my own self knows utter annihilation.'

If we are honest, most of us feel the need to be liked for who we are, at least by the majority of our folk. To flourish requires feeling loved, accepted and happy within the environments where we serve, for this is where others will feel the spirit of God at work too – healing, creating community and urging us onwards to be agents of transformation in the world. The fact remains that if our flock don't like us it's bad news – when the majority are dissatisfied with a leader then the mechanisms of our church organizations tend to grind to an unhappy halt. People continually look to us to represent a variety of characteristics and skills – a notion of holiness, to offer advice, to be capable – and all this can feed our inner vulnerabilities, which tell us that we won't measure up and produce the goods. Clergy have public roles: offering opinions, leading services, assemblies and meetings. We are the face that others critically assess – at times an anathema, at others fond recognition. Like actors and lawyers, we are under pressure to perform, persuade and entertain. I can still remember my insecurity at the beginning of my ordained leadership, seeing quite literally in my mind's eye that 'ideal clergy' person – a capable holy juggler who is invincible and endlessly creative, but definitely not who I felt I was. Even now I sometimes sit in meetings watching speakers and marvel at their self-assured confidence and breadth of knowledge.

Recognizing these pressures, then, how do we retain our own naturalness while keeping up with the rigorous variety of tasks and roles that our jobs require? Perhaps it is helpful to explore how clergy 'unnaturalness' might manifest itself. Our role can be a vulnerable one, and when we feel a lack of affirmation there is the tendency to construct an artificial persona to hide behind, building a protective layer around the individual God originally called. Another way is to appear more knowledgeable or more pious than we actually are, because we feel secretly insecure and anxious about how little we really know. Clergy new to leading services sometimes adopt an overly expressive voice as they speak the liturgy, which results in words that sound false, even funny at times. There is nothing worse than an overemphasized 'pious' voice trying too hard to make everything sound profound or meaningful. As liturgical and worship leaders our charge is to help make the connections with God but not allow ourselves to get in the way in the process. Similarly, we should not bombard others with our own egos and personalities in sermons or groups but share enough of who we are so that it encourages an echo of holy experience within those who are listening.

According to the dictionary definition, something is 'natural' when it contains nothing artificial or does not imitate anything else. Last year I read the inspiring story of Sara Miles, atheist and lesbian, who at the age of 46 walked into a church, took communion and found herself transformed. The experience led her to establish a food bank in her own needy neighbourhood in San Francisco. Her story, *Take This Bread*, is one of the most natural and enthusiastic descriptions of a whole faith journey I have read in a long time. The book is a genuine 'unfolding' of how God takes hold of us and asks us to trust in his working through our lives, however much we think we don't measure up. Miles describes how significant her baptism was, and in the light of this discussion leaders would do well to take themselves back to that moment in their own lives. It is in baptism that we have the assurance of a new birth, where we are remade and clothed in Christ – a point where we are changed and yet remain essentially ourselves. For Miles this becomes a wondrous and terrifying experience in its significance: 'Sometimes I'd felt so uplifted by the thought of becoming special, "marked as Christ's own", that I'd forget I was just one of millions of people making a promise to suffer and to love.'

Our naturalness should rest in the knowledge that we are beautifully unique as well as incomplete and ordinary. Our leadership means relaxing into our own incompleteness. Wilkie Au relates the story of a rabbi who tells a pupil that after each day of creating the world, the Bible states that 'God saw that it was good', except on the sixth day when human beings were fashioned. The conclusion, says the rabbi, is not that human beings are not good but rather that the Hebrew word translated as 'good' in Genesis is better translated as 'complete'. And so we as people remain incomplete always – our calling is to internalize this and work alongside God who slowly but surely fulfils the Christ potential in each of us. Being natural, then, is about working at and enjoying who we are and what we do, being proud of it, but also not leaving things in a static internal place either; we want to avoid falling into the contemporary attitude of stubbornness that demands, 'Well, this is who I am – like it or lump it!'

We model something powerful if we communicate that we are basically comfortable in our human skin as well as our clerical one. This sounds as easy as feeling the summer breeze, yet the reality is that it takes conscious effort to keep remaining so – unaffected by all the insidious temptations to be something we are not that our souls wrestle with. Of course, we may be very good at being priests *naturally* – 'hand and glove' come to mind – because we simply love playing our part in God's ministry or feel very comfortable in being in the 'right place' at a particular time. But others find it much harder to be comfortable in the clergy role, perhaps particularly in places that take us out of our comfort zone.

When we explore into the biblical world of first-century Palestine it's challenging to find an example of a character displaying their 'naturalness' – which is essentially a contemporary and probably Western concept. In a world of complex and subjective personality tests that help us understand ourselves and our working behaviour patterns better, the people who inhabit biblical texts feel two-dimensional – transparently themselves. Yet naturalness in the Bible manifests itself in individuals expressing their emotional life in all of its exuberant and raw state. As we say Morning Prayer each day, for example, we see this modelled through the words of an exultant Zechariah in the Benedictus; he is an elderly and patient father, proudly announcing the special role his son John is to have, preparing the way for the Son of God.

John the Baptist is possibly the New Testament's archetypal ascetic eccentric. Even at the time John was a weird fish – the text tells us he simply appeared in the desert wearing unconventional clothes and eating what might be termed a challenging diet. But John's was a personality that was sincere and authentic, embodied in a role that stated loud and clear his position in the heralding of the reign of God at this point in history. He was unashamed and clear-sighted in his sharp message of repentance and forgiveness of sins. Even in this raw oddness, the text says that the people flocked to him from the countryside, taking him seriously for what he was. And importantly, John refuses to allow the people to misinterpret who he is either. They display confusion, wanting to know his specific identity: 'Are you the Prophet?', 'Are you Elijah?', 'Are you the Messiah?', they ask. John waves all these false personae away – essentially he refuses to mask himself, to pretend to be someone he is not, remaining utterly pure in his self-understanding and intention. By contrast, in several of the Gospel accounts of his ministry, John spits verbal fire at the Pharisees and Sadducees – symbols of religious unnatural-ness and hypocritical piety. Jesus, too, throughout his ministry, was quick to pour down diatribes on these groups, exposing anything that smacked of falseness and insincerity wrapped up as holiness.

Most leaders have a mixture of days when they feel happy and confident in who they are as people and priests, knowing they have delivered well, convincing others of the faith that is as precious as a jewel to them, and others when, like snails, they retreat into shells, hiding behind the symbol of the dog collar or simply choosing not to wear it at all. Being ourselves and celebrating who we are – priest and human being in unique fusion – takes a lifetime to do well. Naturalness can sometimes feel uncomfortable, when we have the courage to be honestly ourselves in all our stark reality and beauty. But those we serve are not stupid either and tend to see through falseness and insincerity. People respond to our honesty and genuineness, even if this is mixed up with imperfection, uncertainty and just 'being strange'.

In many ways Jesus is the archetypal 'natural' leader because he is just himself, pure and simple. He is a Jewish man, respond-ing according to the culture of his time. Jesus, as 100 per cent human as well as divine, had a personality too and we clearly witness this in the stories of the Gospels. He got tired and frustrated, he got angry, he had many compassionate and gen-tle moments, and he was tough and stood up to those who opposed him. Here was a man who was unashamedly himself, most of the time comfortable in his own skin – essentially, just Jesus – no sugar added.

When we cook food made up of natural and pure ingredients, we often have to work harder at tasting it. Our palates have become used to food that is artificially highlighted with flavour. But natural food is better for us, and rediscovering how to be genuine people of integrity who are naturally delighted in God and the richness of life is better for the collective spirituality of our church communities. When I think about it, I tend to accept people as they are. The transvestite who arrives wearing pink nail varnish, the child struggling with behavioural problems, the starchy woman who never encourages my leadership, the flamboyant actor, the reserved lawyer, the millionaires and rough-and-ready farmers – I love them all and believe our churches are richer for the variety and reality of who these folk are and are trying to become. We are called to relish the diversity of people and personalities within the body of the Church. There is a powerful mystery in this and with it comes the model of loving acceptance of our folk, which provides a powerful sign to the world as well. As leader, I need to trust that if I allow people to be themselves naturally, then most of them will help me, with God, to be respected and loved just as 'me' in a similar way. At the 2013 Greenbelt festival Pip Wilson talked movingly about the Church having an opportunity to model a new understanding of 'self-image'. 'You are a beautiful person' is not perhaps a very British way of expressing affirmation, but his aim was for people to accept their imperfect selves and understand themselves, not as a human being but as a human becoming.

Nakedness: facing ourselves with honesty

Most truths are so naked that people feel sorry for them and cover them up, at least a little bit.   Edward R. Murrow

And the man and his wife were both naked, and were not ashamed.   Genesis 2.25

In a busy town centre on a Saturday morning, surrounded by hundreds of shoppers, a Franciscan monk kneels down in the town square and silently prays for the people who live there. Some people mistake him for one of the eccentric street performers who only move when you put money in their collecting basket. Here is a figure considered a freak, as he is pointed at and commented upon; occasionally he is approached by someone genuinely interested in what he is doing there. Although he is clothed completely, in full-length brown habit, his soul is naked as he exposes himself to the wiles of those who pass him by. His ministry is of integrity and vulnerability, as he opens himself entirely to others' misunderstanding and derision, while immersed in a deep trust in God.

His was perhaps something of an extreme calling, but there are times when I have felt a little of this exposure – being interviewed on a radio station and not knowing what questions will be hurled at me, standing in front of 500 teenagers at our local secondary school leading an assembly which I sincerely hope will connect with the lives of the students, or leading a short service in the High Street of our town on Good Friday. At the present time many church communities are feeling something of this communal vulnerability; they are conscious that the Church's internal wrestling over questions such as gay marriage and women in leadership spill over, potentially impacting others who are asking questions of our body.

Most of us, at some point in our lives, have woken up in a cold sweat from a nightmare in which people could see us naked. According to psychologists it indicates a fear of being exposed, of our deepest, darkest secrets being laid bare. As adults we are often uncomfortable with the idea of nudity, even on the beach. Embarrassed, sometimes ashamed of our all too imperfect bodies, we find comfort and protection in being enveloped in clothes. Naked equals a primal state where there is nowhere to hide. As clergy we wear a clerical 'uniform', at least for some of the time. Our clerical shirts, cassocks and albs identify our office and function as well as providing a sense of ceremonial occasion and liturgical drama. Such clothing is double-edged. Psychologically there is one more layer between the 'out-there' stuff and how we might be feeling inside, while our dress potentially lays us open to the diatribes of others (although it can also create opportunities).

For some, such dress enables them to become 'the priest', laying aside the person that they are without it. Our dog collars herald the gospel and hide the scared and unprotected parts of ourselves.

Statistically, clergy tend to be introverts, but the nature of our work requires us to respond to situations in ways that come more easily and naturally to extrovert people. Clergy are constantly managers and chairpersons, as well as being at the front as worship leaders and speakers; and we often have to think on our feet when invited to respond to the unpredictable. With elements of persuasion and performance, the clergy have links with both the legal and the dramatic professions. While most of us, it is hoped, enjoy some of these inevitable perform-ance aspects, there are many folk, like me, who sometimes feel nervous and vulnerable in the public domain, in spite of being competent and articulate. With this often comes an audience's assumption and expectation that we will be extemporaneously expert and convincing about the holy matters with which we are entrusted. It is sometimes taken for granted that we find such a public persona easy.

In her ground-breaking book *Quiet: The Power of Introverts in a World That Can't Stop Talking*, Susan Cain liberates the Western world from the assumption that an extrovert way of behaviour is always good. Her thorough exploration of how introverts can survive in an often aggressively extrovert world provides an alternative model of leadership and power that feels refreshing and much needed. Cain sheds light on the reality that so many of our educational methods focus on forcing essentially introverted people to operate and lead in a way that feels deeply unnatural for them. As a priest I can identify with some of this, and find helpful her advice about how to be an effective small yet insistent voice, by using what she describes as 'soft power'. I often assume that I am required to be hugely extrovert, whereas in actuality many people physically recoil from the bouncy vicar, either because they are introverts themselves or they feel the threat of inner exposure, and vulnerability too. Our churches are full of folk who feel naked inside just as we might do, and to be bombarded with gregarious certainty, or even over-hearty welcome, is not helpful for them.

Sociologists these days recognize that many of us find it difficult to trust or rely upon verbal assurances or bureaucratic systems. In many work environments leaders are encouraged to be vulnerable with those they have responsibility for. Behind this is the belief that trust will be established when employees gain a sense that their managers are people of genuine integrity, even in a climate of intense job insecurity. But it's more than this as well. Part of our calling as Christians is to offer the world our vulnerability, just as Christ did, rather than trying to hide behind the illusion of competence and constant success. We are called to be in touch with and utilize our vulnerability appropriately; we need to find a way in which we can lead out of the vulnerability we feel on a daily basis, due to the weight of the challenges before us and wondering whether we are indeed up to the job. There are inappropriate times and places to use this, of course, along with our own often tightly bandaged brokenness. Such vulnerability is closely aligned to the idea of being honest and assailable in all our encounters.

In John 16.13 Jesus tells his followers: 'When the Spirit of truth comes, he will guide you into all the truth.' God is theological truth, but this verse is also about the power of undiluted honesty. The Holy Spirit is a power who guides us onwards into right situations, if we can trust it rather than insisting on prescribed answers to spiritual questions. As Harry Williams says in *The True Wilderness*, such words are terrifying in their implication of how we approach our faith and work. He warns us against being seen as experts: 'We speak of the expert as somebody who has mastered the subject. And where there is mastery, there is no sense or risk of feeling the danger.' This dynamic can keep other people at emotional arm's length; they feel they cannot come with their own questions of anxiety or theological doubt. The same principle applies if we continuously give the impression that we are shiny, sorted-out people. Naturally folk expect their priests to be stable and emotionally secure enough, but vulnerability as a priest means working at not allowing others to pressurize us into being who they believe we should be; there is power potentially in the idea of 'competent incompetence'. Harry Williams describes this brave approach to leadership:

> As far as I am concerned, the chief work of the Holy Spirit is to reconcile what I think I am with what I really am, what I think I believe with what I really feel; to liberate what fear compels me to suffocate, to introduce the me I loathe and fear and cut dead, to introduce this very me to the glorious liberty of the children of God.

Good leadership emerges out of the context where we find ourselves, hopefully after much listening. But if our exposed humanity can provide the rich soil from which our leading originates, then this becomes a brave and unorthodox model for those who look to us for spiritual, theological and emotional progress.

The contemporary video artist Bill Viola concentrates on the depth and intensity of human emotions. His work seeks to capture human vulnerability and soul nakedness in moments that have the potential to change or reorient our lives. These moments are presented as visual 'stills' or slow motion films where people are seen captivated by an overwhelming experience, their inner states being laid bare. Emotional nakedness is on view before the spectators, paradoxically jagged and posed, spontaneous and yet strangely staged. Viola's work also explores the religious and spiritual significance of biblical stories. His 'Observance' of 2002 shows a solemn line of people who are clearly witnessing a shocking or tragic event; we, as observers of them, do not know what it is. Cynthia Freeland, in an essay on Viola's work, describes how the simple experience of observing this video installation resulted in her weeping uncontrollably, as she made a connection between what she was viewing and a challenging experience she was living through at the time. What is interesting here is that the experience of being confronted with visual vulnerability echoed something within Freeland that released a very real emotion as she contemplated the work. In her own words, she says that 'works like this have such extraordinary verisimilitude they are affecting even when one knows that the participants are actors'. The vulnerability portrayed is beautiful, painful and mysterious, and Viola's work incorporates the human experience of the mystical – a phenomenon that cannot ultimately be portrayed. In his work weighty and precious emotions are not locked within but 'extend beyond persons to colour their world'. The inner states of those portrayed are naked, laid bare at that precise moment, and this has the power to resonate with real emotions, affecting the inner states of those who view them. It is the power of the echo. Likened to the contemplation found in Renaissance paintings, his work establishes a kind of universal connection between both historical and contemporary human experience.

Another story that has the potential to touch us as observers is that of Mary anointing Jesus with expensive perfume, prior to his Passion and death in John 12. In Luke 10, we recall that when Jesus was at Martha and Mary's home, Mary sat at his feet and was commended for it (10.42). Now she embarks on a more scandalous act of reverence by becoming physically intimate with Jesus at a public gathering, wiping his feet with her hair. Even in our culture of open demonstrativeness and relaxed behaviour between the sexes, an act of equivalent intimacy would be unusual. In the world of first-century Judaism we should not underestimate its effect. There can be no doubt that Mary makes herself and her potential reputation very vulnerable. Such self-exposure opens her out to the criticisms of others – here Judas the treasurer – who accuses her great waste, pouring out nard worth at least a year's wages.

But while Mary's act is one of daring boldness, she accomplishes it with utter composure. In contrast to the woman who gatecrashes Simon's respectable dinner party in Luke 7, Mary knows what she is doing and her moment feels premeditated, carefully chosen. There are no histrionics, but inevitably what she does provokes a reaction from those who cannot handle the disgrace of a Jewish woman touching a man's feet with her hair. This particular action would have been considered not only improper but shocking in its erotic overtones: Jewish women did not wear their hair loose in public, let alone use it to touch a male body. Some commentators say that Mary does not fully understand the implications of her actions in this incident, and the text does not explain why she does it in the first place, but Jesus offers an interpretation to those who witness it. What matters is that Mary expresses something of her inner state, in utter nakedness, and through this others are enabled to understand more profoundly the significance of who Jesus is. In addition, Jesus enables connections to be made through putting some interpretation into the moment. Like Viola's stills, here are people caught up in a life drama that has immense spiritual weight. Salvation history is being played out even if those involved do not fully understand the significance of what they do or say. Through her vulnerability, Mary shows those gathered something of God, even though she is criticized by Judas (in John), by the people (in Mark) and by the disciples (in Matthew).

The implication for us in all this is that we too must choose our moments to reveal our nakedness as leaders, for vulnerability is costly. It is not about baring our souls or wearing our hearts on our sleeves continuously, just as Mary did not pour out expensive perfume every day. Our vulnerability is precious, and the 'telling of truth' with integrity takes guts, just as it did for her. Nakedness is about using the hidden parts of our own history and the sharing of our present experience. If we can do so appropriately, perhaps it will release others to do the same, particularly if a new spirit within our community is needed. We can try to enable others to understand that the journey of the spirit is complicated rather than smooth and prescribed – that even those who lead do not always either hold the answers or have the energy that is constantly required. As Mary found, sometimes this laying bare proves to be profoundly uncomfortable both for ourselves and for those who are the recipients.

There is something both stunning and unnerving in the paintings of Lucien Freud: his unclothed bodies and stark expressions stare out, unashamed, from their almost photo-realistic nudity. We must make sure that our vulnerability is used in a similarly honest way, to enable people to see God more clearly, rather than it becoming a subtle form of narcissism. Angela Ashwin, in her book *Faith in the Fool*, recounts stories of the unusual, apparently foolish behaviour of some saints. In the sixteenth century Basil the Blessed walked naked around the streets of Moscow, aiming at recapturing the innocence of Eden so that he could practise being impervious to the derision of onlookers. St Symeon of Emesa rushed naked into the women's section of the public baths in order to be perceived as immoral. Symeon lived in chastity throughout his life but decided upon this course of action in order to avoid any adulation as a holy man. Nowhere is this vulnerable nakedness demonstrated more profoundly than in Jesus on the cross. Here is power given up, worldly success failed, here is utter openness for the sake of love. But such nakedness enables the rough thief hanging next to him to recognize the Son of God, and he is assured of his place in paradise. It enables the centurion looking on from below, a person from a radically contrasting world, to exclaim, 'Truly this man was

God's Son!' (Mark 15.39). Our own soul nakedness is unlikely ever to require such a sacrifice but we can nevertheless model it on Christ's unashamed and sacrificial exposure. We can try using it tentatively to unlock the armour others encase themselves in.

9

Quality of Mind

Thirst: drinking from the well

Our artificial distinctions between the secular and sacred did not matter to Jesus, because he was a mystic. He knew that the way we relate to anything ultimately determines how we relate to everything – including God.

Robin Meyers, *Saving Jesus from the Church*

To live is the rarest thing in the world. Most people exist, that is all. Oscar Wilde

Last summer our family had a big holiday. Blowing money on what probably should have been my pension fund, we journeyed to three countries in the Far East. I hadn't been out of Europe for years, and my children had never been anywhere where genuine culture shock might be involved, and on our return I realized how much I had missed the stretching that travelling can provide. Our trip was fast-paced and varied. We took tuk-tuks to temples in the jungle, rode elephants and visited genocide museums. We ate crocodile and barracuda, witnessed the effects of the notorious chemical Agent Orange, gave our money away to street kids and swam in tropical seas. The experience felt like a rich banquet eaten every day, at the time a little indigestible, but afterwards I knew I would soon be boring my congregations with travel stories that were hopefully related to the things of God. On reflection I recognized that I had been hungry and thirsty to live this kind of adventure once again; it was an experience that resonated with the exhilaration of my youth when I lived and

126

worked in a variety of places around the world. All in all, a short period of immeasurable satisfaction.

As clergy we are challenged to be continually creative, finding new spins on old stories, offering fresh perspectives on time-worn theological concepts and themes. A couple of years ago I began to feel spiritually and intellectually dry, and that I needed to kick-start my approach to both leading worship and theological reading. I stumbled down from the pulpit one Sunday thinking, 'That really was a boring sermon.' These days we feel the pressure to be entertaining and super-meaningful with the gospel message we are called to offer. In his book *The Life and Work of a Priest*, John Pritchard uses the metaphor of the artist: 'The priest is someone who has been dazzled by the beauty of God and longs to reveal the beauty in the world.' He talks about God as the supreme Artist, who invites us into his studio, who gives us the paints and brushes but allows us to paint the canvas in our own way, with our own freedom. 'And so we get on with the great commission . . . painting "after the style of Christ" – the Artist's equally gifted Son. In every church in the world, in every locality and in each life, the paint-ing goes on.' But genuine creative people know about writer's and artist's block; and clergy know about exhaustion and the debilitating nature of doubt, which creeps into our tired souls, disquieting our faith and disabling our ability to enjoy what we offer to others.

Part of this is about making a concerted effort to not become a boring person. We are called to priesthood and leadership with our whole being, bringing our past, offering our present reality, but we need enough sustenance for the future journey too. As leaders we have to learn what *we* need to keep ourselves fed and watered, humanly and spiritually. This involves keeping our theological reading and study up to date, of course (I have started taking the *Church Times* again!) but also allowing ourselves time to experience those things that feed our some-times starved hearts and minds. Whether this is golf or gliding, baking or just going to the pub, we need to know who we are as human beings first and foremost, what keeps us nourished, and where to find it, depending on what stage we are at in our life and work context.

It's also about the attitude we have to our own life and ministry. It's easy to fall into the trap of seeing those things we enjoy as 'extras' that we have to diary-in, rather than experiences we can use to reflect theologically. *Managing Clergy Lives*, a detailed study compiled by Nigel Peyton and Caroline Gatrell, takes into account some honest as well as disturbing facts about when clergy do not include this refreshment in their schedule. While some clergy are obviously able to maintain a healthy equilibrium between work and leisure, and remain clear about the indispensability of time off, in others resentment can build: for example, parishioners can perhaps lazily forget that clergy need space away from the parish, with an 'I know it's your day off but . . .' attitude. Stories in the press talk about clergy hiding in the back rooms of the vicarages, curtains drawn and lights out, oppressed by the doorbell, pretending they are not in. This is not a good situation, and it highlights the complicated relationship of so-called 'work–life' balance that clergy have to manage. Because the vicarage is both workplace and home, the challenge becomes more acute, especially as clergy are usually highly conscientious, offering at least 100 per cent of themselves if not 120 per cent. Ministry is wearying, invigorating, sometimes daunting and at times crushingly tedious. Yet few clergy choose to leave ordained ministry permanently, holding within themselves an inherent belief that they are called to do what they do and refusing to give up. In ministry as 'marathon and not sprint' it is imperative that we find the time to do the things that bring us enjoyment, refreshment and life.

As clergy we can potentially model for others a good and healthy use of time, as well as finding meaning as we do so. In a previous church I worked in, the staff team rethought the theological philosophy for the church, and the concept we prayed through and discussed endlessly was 'Fully Human, Fully Alive'. This means taking seriously the fact that we need rest and recreation in order to rejuvenate as human people. And using these experiences to potentially interweave with our ministerial life can enrich what we do in ministry too, be it reading a quality novel, enjoying a trip to the theatre or being involved in a conversation over a meal with friends. The so-called wasting of time is spiritually crucial; it is often in these fallow moments, when our minds are genuinely resting, that our powers of creativity are most productive. As clergy we should be seen to use our time well, by modelling not working excessively, and be seen to have leisure activities – which can give others permission to enjoy their lives as well. As people who 'give out' much, our spirits need refreshment, even though we will sometimes feel the gaze of parishioners who think we should be working more.

The film *The Best Exotic Marigold Hotel* has as its narrative the fortunes of a group of new retirees who are game enough to risk a new life at a retirement hotel in India. All these people have their personal reasons for making such a momentous decision. Once they get to India they respond in different ways to the riot of noise and colour that is their new environment. Graham Dashwood is in search of a significant former lover, and cannot rest until he has exhausted the possibility of meeting this man again. In the process he allows India to dazzle and delight. Jean Ainslie, by contrast, is anxious and negative about where she finds herself and becomes terrified of even stepping outside of the hotel, which has been a huge disappointment to her preconceptions. 'What do you see that I don't see?' she asks Graham, a man she admires. 'The colour, the light, the smiles, the way that people see life as a privilege rather than a right,' is his response. God offers every human person life, but we are each given the freedom to respond to it in any way we choose. As Christian leaders we present something powerful to the world if we can communicate life's intoxicating beauty and wonder: to revel, embrace and immerse rather than to reject or be frugal with ourselves in terms of our own development and sustenance. It could be said that for too long the sacred and the secular have been compartmentalized; faith, and engendering it in others, is about ourselves allowing the stuff of life to be absorbed into the people we are. We should aim to permit the things we enjoy to feed us, delight us, challenge us, and for these to be 'banked' within us so that they provide a continuous resource on which we can draw, like an evolving and continual theological reflection.

In John's Gospel, chapter 4 shows us Jesus having a clear human need; he is tired and physically thirsty. He asks a Samaritan woman for a drink – something he perhaps ought not to have done, as she is of a race considered unclean, foreign and unacceptable to the average Jew of the time. After an initial conversation, Jesus makes connections between the well and what it is used for literally, moving on to a more metaphorical discussion about what he can offer to her as 'living water'. Throughout, Jesus answers the woman's tentative questioning in a way that sparks her interest. By the end of the conversation she is mesmerized by him and what he is describing: 'Sir, give me this water, so that I may never be thirsty or have to keep coming here to draw water.' Here we witness Jesus taking an earthy and everyday experience, which then leads into an introduction about divine reality, followed by an extended and tangled conversation about husbands and ancestors, and more questions. All this comes from the simple experience of drawing water from a well to drink. Through it all, this woman from Samaria catches a glimpse of the extraordinariness of the person that Jesus is and the rich life that he offers. But before we reach this point, Jesus has presumably refreshed himself (as she and her family do daily), and from this flows something that can be offered in a different form to another person. The episode ends with the woman leaving her water jar and returning to the city she had come from, signifying a life-changing encounter. The water jar is the important point of reference and means of gaining refreshment, but it is ultimately put on one side as her priority becomes revealing to others her encounter with Christ. The important point in this discussion is that she is inquisitive, showing openness to the life that God brings, which is embedded in the existential stuff of human life itself, symbolized here in the drawing and drinking of water. Jesus and this woman have both been thirsty; they leave the encounter physically as well as spiritually refreshed and enlightened.

'Water of Life' is a sculptural water feature by artist Stephen Broadbent situated in the cloister gardens of Chester Cathedral. It describes this life-changing encounter between Jesus and the woman of Samaria. The figures of the two protagonists are connected, brought face to face, giving the work an intimate tenderness and intensity. The figure of Christ cradles a cup in his hands, and water flows from this over into the trough below. The sculpture, commissioned in 1994, is a physical and profound reminder that the everyday experiences of life connect us with God and provide refreshment. George MacDonald describes this juxtaposition of the ordinary experience with the spiritual in a wonderful contemplation of water itself: 'The water itself, that dances and sings, and slakes the wonderful thirst ... this lovely thing itself, whose very wetness is a delight to every inch of the human body in its embrace – this water is its own self, its own truth, and is therein a truth of God.'

The much quoted words of Jesus in John 10.10, to 'have life, and have it abundantly', have precisely this meaning. Few people stop to think that clergy work involves thoughtfulness, time, research and exhaustive creativity. Ministerial work is demanding, in spite of the help given by often excellent and dedicated lay people, and good resources. But thirst and hydrating ourselves is much more than this – it's about the restoring and satisfaction of our whole selves continuously – it's about caring for ourselves pastorally and making time for things that reset our humanity's balance once again. It might be as simple as a glass of wine in front of *Downton Abbey*, or it might mean a big holiday, or just a whole day out walking or fishing. Take the image of those spontaneous fountains in town centres, which periodically spurt out of the ground, providing cool and wet refreshment for frazzled shoppers on a hot day. Children and overheated pets dance delightedly and unselfconsciously in the sprays, enjoying the opportunity to celebrate the delight that can be our life.

So much of what we do as clergy in terms of feeding others centres on the symbolism and reality of the Eucharist. Here we stand, aware that we need Jesus to remind us that we are sustained through the re-enactment of bread and wine – his physical body and blood – the past memory and present reality. Here is perpetual sustenance for souls. Jesus' ministry was a juggling act too, stressful, varied, tortuous at times; but he took himself out and away at times, and immersed himself in the very stuff of life, spending time with friends and those with whom he could be truly himself. But as John Pritchard puts it, 'the days of innocence are over' for those of us who lead. We do no one any favours if we are simplistically sacrificial, if we do not take ourselves and our own human nourishment into account. The cost of serving God in today's climate is nothing other than immense. Our responsibility is to recognize our thirsty humanity and to identify the things that satisfy and quench, so that our inner and outer life remains vital and our personhood is one of balance and perspective.

'Monument to Change as it Changes' is an installation by the American artist Peter Wegner situated at Stanford University in California. It is based on the flip digit module used on the large screens at railway stations that enable travellers to find train times and platform numbers. Wegner's installation shows over 2,000 of these modules, each with 80 colours screen-printed on to a variety of mediums. With similar technology each piece becomes an animated wall of continuous and ever-changing colour. The artist says of the work, 'There is no moment of resolution; just when you think it's arrived somewhere, that it's reached its destination, it sets off again, and it's never static.' I see my life as a priest, and as a human being, a bit like this. With a continual thirst and love for life and what I can learn, my humanity before God should never be static but communicate a kind of holy and colourful vibrancy and enthusiasm. A thirst for life and for God keeps the quality of our minds lively and alert and calls us to respond to the life of the Spirit in a multiplicity of experiences.

Creativity: water and wine

Creativity is not the finding of a thing, but the making something out of it after it is found.   James Russell Lowell

You are not here merely to make a living. You are here in order to enable the world to live more amply, with greater vision, with a finer spirit of hope and achievement. You are here to enrich the world, and you impoverish yourself if you forget the errand.
                                                                                Woodrow Wilson

One of the methods underlying much primary school teaching today is the interdisciplinary process of seeing how a theme can be applied creatively to a multitude of subjects. At our local church school I was, inevitably, the governor responsible for RE and its development for a couple of years, and was invited one day to observe a lesson. The children were learning about the story of Jesus and his disciples being caught up in the storm on the Sea of Galilee. Their teacher encouraged them to act out the story, exploring the emotions the disciples might have experienced when the squall happened. A giant boat was installed in one corner of the classroom, which also doubled up as their 'quiet corner'. The theme of the sea, with the life it sustains, its beauty and its cruel potential for devastation, was woven into most subjects that term and became evident in the art and poetry displayed on classroom walls.

Creativity is built into our very identity as Christian people, even if it lies buried underneath other more pressing concerns. Whenever we create anything beautiful, delicious, thought-provoking or inventive, whenever we do anything well, we participate in the activity of our ultimate creator God, which is not only historical but continuous. Our church foundations are built on the skilled craftsmanship of artists, architects and stonemasons, among others, who produced buildings whose beauty will never be equalled. At the time of writing, the east window in York Minster is undergoing major renovation, and even the observation of this process for those visiting has been imaginatively managed, providing the opportunity to see close up some of the stories within these vibrant and intricate panels.

Sometimes in church life there can be a tendency to understand creativity too narrowly. Sometimes when the 'c word' is mentioned I notice people turn an inward shade of pale. There is an assumption that 'being creative' is more specific than it has to be – that it's about being musical or artistic, which can churn up demons from negative school experiences with all their baggage of non-affirmation. We may bring specialized creative talents to our ministry as leaders, but being creative is much more about cultivating an environment where creativity can flourish and be celebrated. Within our congregations and the groups that we coordinate are people with talents to offer that we do not have ourselves. Sometimes these ministries are specific and unusual. I worked with Simon Buckley for a while (recently featured in the *Church Times*), priest and puppeteer-extraordinaire, who creates puppet characters for both churches and commercial ventures. One of our Readers is a professional storyteller who can bring the biblical text to life in ways I never can, using interactive methods to animate our continuously clamouring boredom.

These days there is an expectation that we should be entertained in church just as we are elsewhere, and a demand that worship and anything church-related is lively and interesting. But it is important to unpack the distinction between being 'entertaining' and being 'creative', because they are not the same. True creativity involves making connections with others in their faith, as well as drawing out people's creativity. Entertainment might have the 'feel-good' factor about it temporarily, but it often keeps those experiencing it in a state of passivity and inaction, as spectators rather than participants.

The criterion of Quality of Mind explores with ordination candidates whether they have sufficient intellectual capacity to undergo a period of theological study and to make sure that they are committed to lifelong learning and ministerial formation. Many candidates are of intellectual high calibre, some of them able to tick the box of being future theological educators. But the most important part of this criterion is the formation of leaders who are able to reflect well theologically and enrich others' experience of faith – people who can make the connections between faith, contemporary culture and the experience of life. New training programmes, such as the St Mellitus course, do this by providing opportunities for theory to run alongside the practice of ministry. The words of the 1662 Prayer Book intercessions ask that 'all Bishops and Curates . . . [may] by their life and doctrine set forth thy true and lively Word'. The word 'lively' is an interesting one because it implies that we need to ignite the word of God with life – that even though the word is already inspired, we have a contribution to make even with our impaired and partial vision. As clergy we are in the business of reverently reinventing and making relevant the truths about God and the history of wisdom entrusted to us as part of our call.

I'm a bit of an amateur artist and for the past few years I've created an installation in our church during Passiontide as an attempt to engage people with the theological concepts surrounding this most momentous of times. Themes like the atonement and resurrection, and questions such as 'Why did Jesus have to suffer?' are not always the easiest for people to get their heads round, especially for newer Christians. But the themes of betrayal, human suffering, sacrifice and new life that underpin these events can be clearly understood.

Two years ago I made a sculpture entitled 'Vicious Circle'. Pieces of jagged broken glass were embedded within 33 rings of painted white concrete, creating a large and visual contemporary crown of thorns. The circle was installed carefully in one of our side chapels (with plenty of health and safety warnings). The pieces of glass were painted in the visceral colours of blood and bruising. Even people who claimed they don't understand modern art nevertheless engaged with the concept of 'the vicious circle' – something of a pattern of destructive behaviour that is a universal experience. The 'Vicious Circle' project explored four characters within the narrative of the Passion who each found themselves in something of a vicious circle: Peter (through lying), Pilate (in the need to be popular), Judas (through greed and power), and Mary (in the love of a parent who ultimately has to let go of control). In the process of forming the sculpture, I asked 30 people I knew what they considered their own 'vicious circle' to be, and they wrote their poignant answers anonymously on specially produced postcards which were then displayed. The installation was used with a variety of services and groups, which aimed at exploring this concept within the story of Jesus' journey to the cross, and also in our own lives. In conclusion, 'Vicious Circle' was used to discuss whether faith can help people break out of unhelpful patterns of behaviour – a risky but real debate. It was a creative attempt to bring to life this challenging Gospel event, making genuine resonances with our lives but ultimately moving us from our individual stories into God's story, something that the Bible continuously asks us to do.

All sincere creativity, whether it is 'home-grown' or 'professional', involves risk, pushes boundaries and involves breaking out of established ways of seeing and understanding in order to change the perspective of our vision. Our country is a diverse one and we who lead church communities find ourselves in a variety of social contexts. Listening to the culture of the context where we are at any given time and discerning how the gospel is best accessed and understood is the beginning of such a creative process. One clergy friend lives in a parish where academic ability, articulate speech and the written word are not strong attributes of his folk. But he is a leader who thinks creatively, outside the box, and part of his approach involves devising simple ways of marking significant events in the church year in ways that do not terrify the people that he serves. To mark the 400th anniversary of the King James Bible he sourced 400 small votive candles, and asked parishioners and others in the local community to come up with their favourite Bible verse or short passage, which most could do. These were collected and each was stuck on to a candle. The candles were arranged in the shape of a large cross and were lit as the central feature for a special service to mark the importance of the Bible in our tradition. The project was given the name of 'A Light Under Our Feet'. Simple, interactive and non-threatening for both clergy and congregation, it was an event that powerfully cele-brated an important milestone in church history. Creativity, then, can in this way be quite simple, and it is helped if it is also 'catchy'. In an earlier chapter we recognized that life for many of us is almost oppressively busy. Creativity can be made particularly attractive if the interactive involvement remains simple and accessible for people to engage with. If such parti-cipation can extend outwards to incorporate others in the local community as well – those who have tentative links with the church – then this becomes a mission activity too.

In the story of the wedding at Cana from chapter 2 of John's Gospel, Jesus becomes the man we would all like to have at our parties. He is not only the practical solution to an immediate crisis, he also provides the symbolic enrichment that such an occasion needs, as a result of changing gallons of water into delicious, aromatic wine. In this story the water can be understood as representing the gospel we already have – an ever-present source of spiritual vitality that constantly underpins and flows through all our ministries. As Christian leaders we are entrusted with this water, but we are asked to transform it, through the power of the Holy Spirit, into something stronger and richer – the wine that fills and fortifies the lives of others and heartens dejected spirits. In our time, having the tools to interpret the biblical text creatively becomes even more vital in both Church and world.

In France the tradition at mealtimes is to drink water alongside wine. At Cana, Jesus tells the stewards to fill the jars with water first. Corresponding to this, then, is the 'staple' of the biblical text and everything that includes our intellectual tradition, which must be a constant resource and reference point for all ministry. We see that Jesus has the basic tools in place before he does anything further with them. In the same way, having good 'quality of mind' requires leaders knowing 'the basics' of the doctrines and history of the Christian faith. Jesus then asks that some of the water be poured out to give to the master of the banquet, who tastes it and is amazed – it is now not water but has been changed into something extraordinarily good. The dynamic happening here is familiar from the plethora of competitive cookery programmes on television, which communicate the desire to make food as innovative and luscious as possible. Food can be 'just food', but if we consider the creativity involved in the complex combinations of ingredients and how they are prepared an interesting analogy can be made with how we mould and shape the knowledge entrusted to us and the platform our office gives us to reflect on it verbally.

But in this story we also find simplicity. Jesus is Jesus, of course, with all his divine power, but essentially all he does is fill the jars with water, which miraculously becomes wine. Our creativity comes from our Creator too, and while we cannot physically turn water into real wine, we do not have to burden ourselves with undue pressure to be all-singing and all-dancing, or believe that we need large amounts of money or people power to put on special events or employ community artists. We don't always require as many resources as we might think in order to communicate effectively to those we find ourselves among. For the past few years our parish has used the Lent courses devised by Hilary Brand, which employ the media of film and literature to provide a gateway to explore spiritual themes relevant to this time of year. These days, then, we don't necessarily have to think things up ourselves; but creativity is about being resourceful with the tools available so that we can continuously refresh the gospel with a new palette of colours. We might feel that we don't always do this very well: while water is the great elixir of life in the Bible, wine did not flow so readily. The poor would have drunk little wine, and a costly celebration such as the wedding at Cana would for many people have meant saving hard to pay for it. Running out of wine would represent instant shame for the hosts. We perhaps feel a little like this at times, embarrassed or upset because we fall short, not providing enough interest and sustenance for our folk, week in and week out.

Earlier this year I took my son to see the band Stomp, the electrifying British group who make percussive music using everything from brooms, oil drums and Zippo lighters to kitchen sinks. They use ordinary and often discarded objects to create something extraordinary, enriching and deeply satisfying to experience. Innovative music is produced from a combination of unusual objects and the band members' creative talent, which has its roots in the poor communities of township and ghetto. The changing of the water into wine at the wedding at Cana is about revealing the hidden awesomeness of Jesus at an ordinary domestic event. The story tells us that the power of God can be seen and heard through the commanded words of Jesus. Having an integral 'quality of mind', then, is to take our own life-giving and ordinary tools and offer them constantly as good food and new wine to people who are eager to be enriched by the nature and activity of God.

I have always liked the idea of creating an 'enchanted space' – a physical or mental place where others might just catch a glimpse of the numinosity and mystery of God. Some might stumble over such supernatural overtones, but there is something powerful about experiencing God in places where we are spellbound and fascinated by creativity. My own faith was rebuilt through the experience of wandering around the two buildings that constitute Coventry's cathedrals. The juxtaposition of the destroyed and charred with the glorious new, full of works of art, represented for me a place of true 'enchantment'; I was drawn back to understanding the healing love of God once again. We are called to create environments where creativity is alive, accessible and fluid, enchanted spaces where people can bring their own creativity to blossom and make it into wine. Like Coventry Cathedral, the wedding at Cana creates a sign of newness; it's interesting that this passage is often read at the beginning of the year, on the second Sunday after Epiphany. The Cana story invites those who preach and teach, as well as those who hear, to reflect on creativity as a phenomenon that establishes the new, the imaginative, the engaging and the relevant, so that, in the words of Gerard Sloyan, 'There must be newness of life in the many places where Christians assemble if this is not to be an idle winter's tale.'

Bibliography

Books

Angela Ashwin, *Faith in the Fool*, London: Darton, Longman and Todd, 2009.

Wilkie Au, *By Way of the Heart: Towards a Holistic Christian Spirituality*, London: Geoffrey Chapman, 1990.

Rob Bell, *What We Talk About When We Talk About God*, New York: HarperCollins, 2013.

Dietrich Bonhoeffer, *True Patriotism*, London: William Collins, 1965.

Ruth Burrows, *To Believe in Jesus*, London: Sheed and Ward, 1978.

Susan Cain, *Quiet: The Power of Introverts in a World That Can't Stop Talking*, London: Penguin, 2012.

Christopher Cocksworth and Rosalind Brown, *Being a Priest Today*, Norwich: Canterbury Press, 2002.

Michael Dwinell, *Being Priest to One Another*, Liguori, MO: Triumph Books, 1993.

Robin Greenwood, *Transforming Priesthood: A New Theology of Mission and Ministry*, London: SPCK, 1994.

Margaret Guenther, *Holy Listening: The Art of Spiritual Direction*, London: Darton, Longman and Todd, 1992.

Gustavo Gutiérrez, *On Job: God-Talk and the Suffering of the Innocent*, New York: Orbis, 1986.

Kent Haruf, *Plainsong*, London: Picador, 1999.

Vanessa Herrick and Ivan Mann, *Jesus Wept: Reflections on Vulnerability in Leadership*, London: Darton, Longman and Todd, 1998.

W. R. Inge, *Personal Religion and the Life of Devotion*, London: Longmans, Green, 1927.

Christopher Jamison, *Finding Happiness: Monastic Steps for a Fulfilling Life*, London: Phoenix, 2008.

John Koenig, *New Testament Hospitality*, Eugene, OR: Wipf and Stock, 2001.

Journal of Religion and Film, 'Babette's Feast: A Religious Film by Wendy Wright', Vol. 1, No. 2, October 1997, Omaha, NE: University of Nebraska.

Rosemary Lain-Priestley, *Does My Soul Look Big in This?* London: SPCK, 2012.

John Lees, *Secrets of Resilient People*, London: Hodder, 2014.

C. S. Lewis (compiler), *George MacDonald: An Anthology*, London: Geoffrey Bles, 1946.

Robin R. Meyers, *Saving Jesus from the Church: How to Stop Worshipping Christ and Start Following Jesus*, New York: HarperOne, 2009.

Sara Miles, *Take This Bread*, New York: Ballantine Books, 2007.

Northumbria Community, *Celtic Daily Prayer*, London: Collins, 2000.

Henri Nouwen, *In the Name of Jesus*, London: Darton, Longman and Todd, 1989.

Henri Nouwen, *Reaching Out*, London: Random House, 1986.

Henri Nouwen, *The Wounded Healer*, London: Darton, Longman and Todd, 1994.

Gordon Oliver, *Ministry Without Madness*, London: SPCK, 2012.

Nigel Peyton and Caroline Gatrell, *Managing Clergy Lives: Obedience, Sacrifice, Intimacy*, London: Bloomsbury, 2013.

John Pritchard, *The Life and Work of a Priest*, London: SPCK, 2007.

Michael Ramsey, *The Christian Priest Today*, London: SPCK, 2009.

Richard Rohr, *Hope Against Darkness: The Transforming Vision of St Francis in an Age of Anxiety*, Cincinnati, OH: Franciscan Media, 2001.

Alan J. Roxburgh and Fred Romanuk, *The Missional Leader: Equipping your Church to Reach a Changing World*, San Francisco: Jossey-Bass, 2006.

Philip Sheldrake, *Spirituality: A Very Short Introduction*, Oxford: Oxford University Press, 2012.

Margaret Silf, *Taste and See: Adventuring into Prayer*, London: Darton, Longman and Todd, 1999, reprinted 2000.

Stanley H. Skreslet, *Picturing Christian Witness: New Testament Images of Disciples in Mission*, Great Rapids, MI: Eerdmans, 2006.

Gerard Sloyan, *John: Interpretation: A Bible Commentary for Teaching and Preaching*, Louisville, KY: John Knox Press, 1988.

Richard Stengel, *Mandela's Way: Lessons on Life*, London: Virgin Books, 2010.

R. S. Thomas, 'The Kingdom', from the original poem from R. S. Thomas, *H'm*, London: Macmillan, 1972.

Dave Tomlinson, *How To Be a Bad Christian . . . and a Better Human Being*, London: Hodder and Stoughton, 2012.

Jean Vanier, *Community and Growth*, London: Darton, Longman and Todd, 1979.

Simon P. Walker, *Leading Out of Who You Are: Discovering the Secret of Undefended Leadership*, Carlisle: Piquant Editions, 2007.

Hannah Ward and Jennifer Wild (compilers), *The Lion Christian Meditation Collection*, Oxford: Lion Publishing, 1998.

Hannah Ward and Jennifer Wild (compilers), *The Lion Christian Quotation Collection*, Oxford: Lion Publishing, 1997.

Leslie Weatherhead, *Prescription for Anxiety*, London: Hodder and Stoughton, 1956.

H. A. Williams, *The True Wilderness*, Harrisburg, PA: Morehouse Publishing/Mowbray, reprinted 1999.

Kit Williams, *Masquerade*, London: Jonathan Cape, 1979.

Rowan Williams, *Writing in the Dust: After September 11th*, London: Hodder and Stoughton, 2002.

Resources on artists

Ai Weiwei: <www.aiweiwei.com>; 'Sunflower Seeds' is widely available to view on the internet.

Stephen Broadbent: <www.sbal.co.uk>; 'Water of Life' is widely available to view on the internet.

Antony Gormley: *Antony Gormley* (Contemporary Artists Series), London: Phaidon, 2000. Information about 'Angel of the North' from Gateshead Council website and <www.antonygormley.com>.

'Hospitality' exhibition in Bath Abbey: accompanying publication by Claire Todd, Alan Garrow and Mike Tooby, Bath School of Art and Design, Bath: Wunderkammer Press, 2013.

Liverpool Biennial: <www.biennial.com>.

Bruce Nauman: 'Raw Materials' is widely available to view on the internet.

Tate Modern: <www.tate.org.uk>.

Bill Viola: *The Art of Bill Viola*, edited by Chris Townsend, London: Thames and Hudson, 2004; <www.billviola.com>.

Mark Wallinger: 'The first artist on the plinth' from *Recreative: An Online Community and Resource Exploring Contemporary Art*, <www.recreativeuk.com>.

Peter Wegner: <www.peterwegner.com>.

Rachel Whiteread: her work is widely available to view on the internet.

Other resources

Hilary Brand: Lent courses, written on a variety of films and literature, including *Chocolat*, Narnia and the works of C. S. Lewis, and *The King's Speech* (*Finding A Voice*), London: Darton, Longman and Todd.

Eden Project, Bodelva, Cornwall: <www.edenproject.com>.

Healthy Living Centre: <www.bbbc.org.uk/health-centre>.

Justice Mail, a way for local churches to support working for justice in an accessible way online: <www.justicemail.org.uk>.

St Patrick's Breastplate: <www.prayerfoundation.org/st_patricks_breastplate_prayer.htm>.

Somewhere Else, Liverpool City Centre Methodist Church bread-making project: <www.somewhere-else.org.uk>.

Stomp, dynamic percussion group with a regular London show: <www.stomponline.com>.

Margaret Wheatley, American writer and consultant studying social behaviour: information from 'Warrior of the Human Spirit', *The Intelligent Optimist*, 21 December 2012; <www.margaretwheatley.com>.

Sources of epigraphs and other quotations

Hannah Ward and Jennifer Wild (compilers), *The Lion Christian Meditation Collection*, Oxford: Lion Publishing, 1998.

Hannah Ward and Jennifer Wild (compilers), *The Lion Christian Quotation Collection*, Oxford: Lion Publishing, 1997.

<www.brainyquote.com>.

<www.goodreads.com>.

Lightning Source UK Ltd.
Milton Keynes UK
UKHW020959070521
383312UK00014B/1207